BREAKING OUT

BREAKING OUT

...of a job you don't like

...and the regimented life

by DON BIGGS

David McKay Company, Inc.

NEW YORK

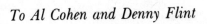

To Al Cohen and Denny Flint

Acknowledgments

I can never fully express my appreciation to the many executives (corporate escapees past and future) and their wives and children who spent many hours with me in candid conversation, and who often took me into their homes for varying lengths of time to experience their lives with them.

I am also indebted to the scores of corporate managers, management consultants, psychologists, psychiatrists, ministers, family counselors, encounter group leaders, executive recruiters, human relations researchers and others who gave of their time, wisdom and good offices in making this book possible.

To these then, and to many others who could not be named, my special thanks: David Bacon, Ph.D.; Esta Belcher; Lee Belcher; Steven Bindeman, Ph.D.; Cdr. Roy A. Black, USN; Harvey Brackbill; Helen Brackbill; Bradley Brewer; George Calminson; Mary Calminson; Rev. Robert Caldwell; Alex Carter; Judy Carter; Walter Chamberlain; Alvin M. Cohen; Beth Cohen; Bernard Haldane; Isaac Harris; Sidney Heilveil; Marshall N. Heyman, Ph.D.; Bruce Hiptak; Rev. Trevor Hoy; Nicholas

Johnson; Ron Kahn; Barton Knapp, Ph.D.; Harold C.
Lyon, Ph.D.; Edith Lyon; Kenneth Malachuck; Trudy
Malachuck; Alice Maser; Conrad Maser; Rev. Robert
Cromey; John W. Costello; Edelen Dawson; Wilbur
Dove; Albert Ellis, Ph.D.; Edward Elkin, Ph.D.;
  Arden A. Flint, M.D.; Rose Mary Flint; Edith Fields;
Eugene Fields; Maurice S. Friedman, Ph.D.; William Gel-
lermann; Eugene T. Gendlin, Ph.D.; Ben Goodwin,
M.D.; Jody Goulden; Joseph C. Goulden; Joyce Graham;
Ralph Graham; Richard Gross, Ph.D.; Rollo May, Ph.D;
Joan McKinney; Cyril Mill, Ph.D.; Louis R. Mobley; Larry
Murphy; Michael Murphy; Rose Murphy; Bill Neely;
Martina Neely; Dena Nye; Max Nye; Connie Holt; Mau-
rice Holt; Edwin Ochs; Lottie Ochs; Carmen Ortiz; Cae-
sar Ortiz; Erdman Palmore, M.D.; Amos Peters; Kather-
ine Peters; Lana Pipes; Francis Pipes; Margaret Powers;
Robert Powers; Rosalie Rathman; Sam Rathman; Pa-
tricia Rice, Ph.D.; J.D. Ritchie; Frederick C. Rockett,
Ph.D.; Carl Rogers, Ph.D.; Irving Schultz; Charles Sea-
shore, Ph.D.; Dennis Shattuck; Elizabeth Shattuck; Her-
bert A. Shepard, Ph.D.; Martin Shepard, M.D.; Sidney
Simon, Ph.D.; Sally Skinner; Everett L. Shostrom, Ph.D.;
Alfred P. Slaner; Lish Southworth, Ph.D.; James
Swander, Ph.D.; Karen Swander, Ph.D.; Kenneth Trog-
den, Ph.D.; Leonard P. Ullman, Ph.D.; Marta Vago,
M.S.W.; Kermit Vandivier; David Viscott, M.D.; Harold
C. Visotsky, M.D.; Myron T. Weiner, Ph.D.; Robert L.
Wells; Ron Wilson; Joan Wolfgang; Wendy Wyatt; Con-
nie Yee; David Youland; Nancy Youland; Anita Gross;
Margaret Hennig.

I shall always be grateful to my good friend Michael
Curtis for his invaluable contribution to the organization
of this book, his review of the final manuscript and for

the insight which directed me to many areas that deserved exploration. My thanks also to Joseph C. Goulden for his encouragment and help along the way.

Finally, my thanks to Sandy Held, Barbara Rubel, Katherine Fleigel, and Eliza Childs for their help in preparing the final manuscript.

Contents

Introduction

The writing of *Breaking Out* and my personal experience
share a common beginning. They were both born on a
February afternoon in the office of a good friend who is
an executive with a major Washington, D.C., trade association.

We had finished our business together and were talking of other things when Ed's face suddenly brightened
and he said, "Don, did I ever show you the pictures of
my new country place?" I said he hadn't, and Ed handed
me a half-dozen snapshots of a striking, contemporary
five-room retreat somewhere in the Virginia foothills.

Huge glass windows soared high above a broad sundeck overlooking a misty valley that had its floor nearly
half a mile below.

Two stone chimneys interrupted the steep slant of a
copper-sheathed roof, and tall, slim windows admitted
slanting vaults of sunlight into the house's several
rooms. High on one end of Ed's new house a sliding
glass door and balcony broke the expanse of unpainted,
gray siding. An open carport under the hillside house
was partially enclosed by an outside stairway leading up
to the sundeck and the house's main entry.

Dogwood and maple and oak and pine trees surrounded the house, which Ed told me was nearly a mile from the nearest road or other building.

Clearly, the house was something Ed was tremendously proud of and not the kind of place he found easy to leave on a Sunday afternoon whose setting sun he would next see rising in the east on his way to work Monday morning.

When I handed the photos back to Ed, he looked at them for a moment, and then the energy and lift I'd seen a moment ago seemed to drain out of him.

He raised his eyes to meet mine. "You know, something's happening to me. This," he said, indicating the paneled office, "used to mean something to me—this office, the job, being on the 'inside' of important things; but I don't get anything out of it now, nor out of much else either.

"I'm pushing fifty and I guess some people might tell me it's male menopause, but I think it's that I am finally mature enough to know better than I did when I was younger and hot to set the world on fire.

"Everything I've worked for seems unreal, as though I could reach out and pass right through it and never feel anything was there."

I asked Ed about quitting and doing something he might like to do; maybe spend more time with his wife, giving up the daily hours of creep-and-crawl auto commuting and the frenzied meetings, often hastily called to counter some real or imagined political threat against the industry his association was expected to protect.

He'd often told me about "too much travel and too many drinks and not enough sleep" which were as much a part of his life as working lunches and a briefcase stuffed with problems.

Though his kids were grown, his home paid for, and he had more money and fewer financial responsibilities than at any time in his life, Ed told me he couldn't quit. "I don't think I could stand the feeling that I'd somehow 'copped out.' " And he couldn't quite accept the idea of moving to another job that would take less out of him. "I know it's stupid, but I'd feel too much like I was 'stepping down' or falling down on the job I'm doing now."

As we talked on, both aware that Ed would never be able to break out of the walls of work and status that had grown up around him, I suddenly saw that my own life-long effort to break into the system had trapped me just as surely as Ed's inability to break out had trapped him.

As long as I can remember I had been split between a driving desire to be part of the group that surrounded me, and a feeling that by striving to be like others I was missing being myself.

My early need for acceptance, particularly acceptance by superiors at work, probably came out of a deep feeling of rejection by my manufacturer father, whose respect I felt could only have been earned by great financial success in business.

Consequently, I sought and gained responsible positions with major corporations, but was never comfortable in the tight, white collar my employers expected me to wear. Nor did I feel room to breathe deeply in a value system that forced me to shape myself to meet corporate expectations of how my family and I should live.

While talking with Ed that afternoon I suddenly envisioned one of those life-size, stiff, plaster-like sculptures that were getting a lot of attention at that time.

In my imagination I saw this completely white room, maybe eight-by-sixteen feet, with a row of white bars running down the middle of the room from end-to-end, separating it into two narrow halves.

At one end, on one side of the bars was Ed, or some-one like him, in white, frozen motion, frantically strain-ing against the bars trying to break through to the other side.

On the other side of the bars, at the opposite end of the room, was me, stark white like Ed, and frozen stiff in my frenzy, desperately trying to break through to the side of the room where he was.

One of us was *in* and one of us was *out,* but we were equally prisoners because neither of us could let go of the bars.

Before I left Ed's office I knew I'd be able to turn away from the bars and walk out of that cell.

Before long, my determined effort to "stop being un-real" brought on a candid confrontation with my boss that cost me my job.

Unlike other men and women in *Breaking Out* who made ready to leave the corporate world, my wife and I were unprepared for the place where we suddenly found ourselves.

We had made no financial preparations for our com-fortable $25,000 annual income to be suddenly stopped. I was forty-four and had been on my current job less than a year, hardly strong selling points when you have to find work fast.

What we did have going for us, though, was almost two years' participation in encounters, Gestalt workshops, and sensitivity training at the human-potential move-ment's "growth centers."

Perhaps it was that background that enabled us to stay out rather than to try staying in, and to set out on our own where earning a living was concerned.

One phase of my work which I'd always enjoyed was writing, and since I was at that very moment very much in touch with having been thrown out of the rat race, I decided to seek out others who had left the corporate world. I wanted to learn how they had solved some of the problems, and how they made the most of new freedoms, and I thought their story would make a pretty good book.

The first thing I discovered when I told friends and former associates that I'd decided to stay "out" was how many people I knew had a secret desire to leave the system themselves.

They provided a list of rather practical reasons for wanting out:

They were wasting too many hours a day commuting. They weren't able to work their best hours, which may have been from 8 P.M. to 4 A.M. They didn't like to be away from their families on frequent business trips. They wanted to have more control over their time, perhaps increased time off as well as more hours to devote to work they loved instead of attending meetings.

They wanted to live someplace other than where their employers wanted them to live. They wanted more control over their futures. They had seen friends, or themselves had been, merged out, maneuvered out, transferred, laid off, furloughed, retired and fired when they didn't want to be.

And finally, they just wished they could be more honest about how they felt and what they thought and the way they wanted to be.

Those didn't seem like very strange values to me. Nobody wanted to go off to a forest and contemplate a tree (at least not full time), and nobody I talked to was eager to go on welfare.

It began to sound like a considerable body of people might like to read about "breaking out."

The individuals I'd talked with first were men and women who *wanted* to break out. How about people who *had* broken out? Maybe they were all off living in caves someplace or were reduced to accepting welfare.

Once I began looking for "escapees," they were easy to find. Everybody knew somebody. People I knew were acquainted with families who'd given up good jobs to make less and live more. There were legions of people on the rolls of human-potential growth centers who'd left the rat race. And the psychologists, psychiatrists, marriage counselors and ministers I interviewed were all able to refer me to people who'd found their own values to live by.

I conducted interviews on tape, using a small recorder from which I transcribed discussions after returning home. Between people still in the corporate system and those out of it, even the sounds were different.

In the background of taped interviews with corporate officials and industrial psychologists and consultants were the sounds of telephones and buzzers and interruptions and (so help me!) an Alka-Seltzer fizzing up and being gulped down.

The background sounds on tapes of people who've broken out tell another story. They are the sounds of pleasure boats moving up and down Florida's inland waterway, of doves (who live in Ben Goodwin's Dallas, Texas, backyard), of children playing (while I talked with Larry Murphy), of a farm tractor's engine echoing across the valley at Bill and Martina's West Virginia country home, and the sound of wind and trees and birds, and an outboard boat somewhere far across the lake (at David and Nancy Youland's Maine hunting and fishing lodge).

The voices were different too. I listened to the vibrations of too many tense vocal cords in executive offices and corporate headquarters around the country. People I interviewed who'd broken out had no reason to make points, or be heard above anyone else, nor could they win or lose depending on how they impressed me. I heard their security when I transcribed what they told me.

To a person, escapees told me they considered themselves unemployable so far as returning to the system was concerned. Even if some of the men would be tempted to try it, their families would never go along. "If my husband ever decided to go back to the corporate rat race," Ron Kahn's wife, Barbara, told me, "much as I love him, he'd have to go alone."

Since this introduction was written after *Breaking Out* was listed in the publisher's catalog, I already have heard from people (newsmen mostly) who ask questions about this book, and there is one they nearly always ask which I can't answer.

"But what would happen to our competitive economic system," they say, "if everybody was free just to go and do his own thing?"

I suspect most of the important jobs would get done. I've talked to people who teach for the love of it, to college graduates who are carpenters, former professionals who work on loading docks, executives who have become ministers, and ministers who have become psychologists and psychologists who have become artisans.

There are engineers who would have stayed at the drawing board had they not felt pressures to accept promotions. The man who photocopied many chapters of this book is a former executive who now runs a Kwik-Copy franchise across the street from one of the eighteen retail chain stores he used to be responsible for. His hours and responsibilities are of his own choosing now.

I don't know how General Motors and General Dynamics would fare, and I am sure there would be a number of changes I am not able to foresee, but I cannot help but believe that while an America populated by people who have "broken out" might not be so rich a nation, it might well be a far happier one.

BREAKING OUT

1

The Corporate Dropouts

More and more Americans are learning what the rich already know—and what mothers have been telling their children for years: that money doesn't buy happiness.

Growing numbers of men no longer have their eyes fixed on the boss's door, waiting for him to move on— or pass on. Though some still strive to "make it" on society's terms, the most pressing need of many others resolves itself into three words, "I want out."

The effects of regimentation on the production line— absenteeism, high turnover, and wildcat strikes—are well documented. But the consequences of regimentation in the executive suite are still barely understood. In a culture that likes to pride itself on smooth waters, the monster that hides in the deeper eddies and currents of the corporate mainstream has been felt more than seen, its victims slowly and silently sucked dry of humor, and emotion, and the ability to feel.

What does the new breed of corporate dropout say

he's escaping from? What does he find once he's walked out on society's idea of success? Are these men misfits and malcontents that the corporate power structure is better off without? If, as some psychologists state, today's executive dropouts are among the best men the business world has ever known, then what's gone wrong with corporate America?

In our nine-month search for some of the answers to these questions, we talked with more than one hundred and fifty corporate executives, former executives, organizational development psychologists and executive recruiters. We interviewed too, many of the "outsiders," psychologists, psychiatrists, ministers, group encounter leaders and marriage counselors who see the price executives (and their families) pay for the success they believe will bring them happiness, recognition, and admiration from their peers.

In certain key respects, the findings of our *on-the-record* interviews with men who've stepped out of the company organization chart were similar to our *off-the-record* talks with executives who feel boxed in by their present positions in the corporate hierarchy. Increasingly, good men give up sizable paychecks and challenging jobs because:

They feel they are slipping away from themselves, caught up in a corporate role that leaves less and less room in their lives for them to be "real."

They resent demands on their "own" time, demands which grow with each promotion until there is practically no line between hours which belong to the company and those which supposedly belong to them.

They see little reason to "bust their guts" for raises that are eaten up by the expectations of rank, by homes, clubs, cars and other possessions which often leave them further in debt with each promotion.

They don't like some of the things they do in the name of profit, things which make them dislike themselves at the end of each working day.

They miss their families. They miss what they used to feel about their wives. They miss being able to do "nothing" without feeling guilty about it.

What executives and former executives tell you, in the sparse words of men used to speaking more in private than for publication, is echoed by management specialists and physicians.

"The ulcer," says Jerome Steiner in *Harvard Business Review,* "is only one of the many symptoms of modern man who has lost touch with himself. As today's business managers move into top positions, they become increasingly prone to interpersonal problems which are reflected in alcohol ingestion, marital instability, sexual maladjustment and physical complaints. . . . At home he may find he has lost the art of contented leisure, communication with his wife and children, and the sure knowledge of the functional capacity of his physical being. . . . He is increasingly pushed to identify himself with the business rather than his own future—a change in goal direction that, in itself, can cause a crisis in identity."

Psychiatrist Erich Fromm would agree. "Many a businessman," says Fromm, "feels himself the prisoner of the commodities he sells; he has a feeling of fraudulency about his product and a secret contempt for it. Most important of all, he hates himself, because he sees his life passing him by without making any sense beyond the momentary intoxication of success. Of course, this hate and contempt for others and oneself, and for the very things one produces, is mainly unconscious, and only occasionally comes to awareness in a fleeting thought, which is sufficiently disturbing to be set aside as quickly as possible."

More and more executives, middle managers, and technical employees are unwilling to join their corporate employers in short-changing or endangering the public, even when blowing the whistle means they're likely to get fired. Others, who don't want to make a federal case out of their employers' chicanery, say it's a matter of having to quit to keep their self-respect.

One engineer for a Houston, Texas area petrochemical producer says he plans to resign as soon as he can find another job. "Not long ago," he told me, "the industry found a way to formulate plastics that break down chemically over a predetermined period of time. After crowing about how it would aid the environment by reducing the amount of trash to be disposed of, the industry started offering this same built-in biodegradability to the manufacturers of plastic waste cans, laundry baskets, children's toys and so on.

"The result of this scientific advance is that people are being sold products which have a deliberately reduced service life and we go on making more trash than ever."

Kermit Vandivier, former B. F. Goodrich data analyst and author of *The Great Aircraft Brake Scandal, (Harper's,* April, 1972) told me he had to go to the Federal Bureau of Investigation to get anything done to stop production on faulty brakes his company was making for the Air Force A-D7 attack fighter. Production was based on fraudulent test reports he and others had been ordered to write.

Vandivier said that when he brought the situation to the attention of a senior executive, he was told, "You're just getting upset for nothing. I just do as I'm told and I advise you to do the same."

A government investigation, initiated on the basis of Vandivier's visit to the FBI, resulted in Goodrich having to replace $70,000 worth of badly designed brakes for the A-D7. The disheartening thing to Vandivier, now a reporter for the Troy (Ohio) *Daily News,* was that the two men involved in the scandal who "went along with" company efforts to cover up the deceit, were soon promoted by Goodrich, "presumably for loyalty." The message delivered by management's action in handing out the promotions is loud and clear.

Time magazine (April 12, 1972) tells of Pfizer, Inc. employees who, according to columnist Jack Anderson, "were urged to write their Congressmen to express opposition to legislation which would establish a federal consumer protection agency." While I was in Texas researching this book, executives at a major oil and refining company told me of receiving notes from management suggesting contributions of "specific dollar amounts" to certain business-oriented political education organizations.

Major corporations don't advertise their losses, and may not know how many of their best men resign simply to be "getting out." In my talks with corporate presidents, though, and with vice presidents of industrial relations and administrators of government agencies, all admitted they'd lost good people during the past year who'd left saying they were simply calling it quits. Organizational psychologists suspect that others leave for the same reasons, though they list family health or teenager problems as their motive for moving to another city.

If newspaper and magazine stories, and appearances of executive dropouts on radio and television talk shows are any indication, the numbers are something to be reckoned with. Almost every newspaper and magazine in the United States has printed feature stories about men, successful and secure by society's standards of achievement, who have quit the corporate world for a slower-paced life of their own making.

The *Wall Street Journal,* in a two-part, front-page series titled "The Great Escape," February, 1971, told the stories of five successful men who resigned from top-paying jobs to raise cranberries, teach skiing, raise sheep, sail around the world, or lay plans for the realization of some other long-repressed dream.

A June 12, 1970, feature in *Life* described the lives of five men who quit jobs with salaries ranging up to $35,-000 a year, to teach Eskimo children in a school north of the Arctic Circle, or work on the loading dock of a department store or, "play the rest of life by ear." *The New York Times, Cosmopolitan, The National Observer, Los Angeles Magazine,* and scores of other publications have run stories about men who've decided that, in spite of an office in the executive suite, they simply weren't making it.

Dun's Review for January, 1971, cites the case of thirty-six-year-old Aldo Bussi and forty-five-year-old Nicholas Sakellarios, former co-workers in the electronics division of a major U.S. corporation. "Bussi and Sakellarios," said *Dun's* article, "had the look of men who had found a home," but suddenly they "ran away from home" to start a small company making electronic components and systems. "If we hadn't left," they told the man from *Dun's,* "we'd have drowned."

Newly promoted to head his company's control electronics department, Bussi helped sales rise from $500,-000 to more than $2 million his first year on the job. But his suggestion of reinvesting profits to develop new products was turned aside by top management which also gave him a "feeling of having no place to go but sideways." Bussi might have stayed to see if he could sell his plan, but corporate nitpicking drove him (and a number of other middle managers) away before he could make his final contribution.

In a September, 1969, article titled "The Revolt of the Middle Managers," *Dun's* described the rumblings of discontent among second-echelon executives stemming from vague unhappiness with the status quo and a desire to "somehow attain more meaning in their corporate life."

"Now, just a year or so later," says a *Dun's* January, 1971, article, "a number of executives are doing something concrete about that disenchantment, and the ferment among middle managers has become so widespread—and so deeply felt—that it has serious implications for every corporation."

Second-echelon managers see themselves as men in the middle in several respects. They aren't high enough to be free of the restraints of organizational orthodoxy, the "petty rituals whose purpose is lost in antiquity," yet they are often expected to carry responsibility without real authority. They worry so much about employer expectations with respect to their life style, that they spend up to the limit of their means to live like executives.

Many middle managers feel their employers demand more from them than corporations have any right to expect. "What the company has to offer," they feel, "isn't that valuable in terms of one's total life."

"Doing the same thing every day for decades is deadening. . . . Fifty acres of land can't stand up to the harassment of being planted in nothing but wheat, and people can't take that kind of harassment. They wither."

—former insurance man

"I wanted to live somewhere I could hike and hunt. . . . I had five small children growing up next to a big sinful city. I really didn't like labor relations. . . . I've met wonderful people here who hold very simple, unimportant jobs. I got a little arrogant when I was at United."

—former United Airlines
    labor relations executive
    who quit for life in the
    Colorado high country

"Organizations oppress you. . . . They hold you down. I felt as if industry were consuming me. It took what it wanted, but didn't put anything back. It doesn't allow one to grow as a person. You can grow in its image, but that's the only way. I don't admire the guy who's president of a company any more. In fact, I feel pretty sorry for him."

—a former corporate
    engineer

A front-page story in the *Wall Street Journal,* May, 1971, gives an inkling of how some corporate kings have arranged their lives. "They run their companies from home or yacht, shun formal clothes, sleep late and do push-ups at board meetings," says the *Journal.*

The king, it seems, manages to live the very kind of life sought by those who desert the corporate world by "breaking out." Martin Stone, forty-three-year-old chairman of the Los Angeles-based Monogram Indus-

tries, often shows up at his office in blue jeans and loaf-
ers, does push-ups during the meetings and tosses a
football around with associates. Arkansas-Louisiana Gas
Co. chairman and president W. R. Stephens arrives in his
office at 6 A.M. and winds up his work by 2:30 P.M. when
he heads for his farm to fix fences or drive a tractor.
"Working with your hands," he says, "helps you work
with your mind."

Forty-two-year-old Advent Corporation president
Henry Kloss, reports the *Journal,* "can be seen any week-
day morning clad in khakis and shirtsleeves as he bicycles
through Harvard Square to his cluttered office in an old
factory building on the Charles River." "It's more conve-
nient for me to come and go with my bike," he says,
"besides, we have only one car and my wife uses it. I hate
possessions. They're just a nuisance."

Elmer Winter, president of a Milwaukee-based tempo-
rary-help firm, Manpower, Inc., often spends his working
hours on a park bench or walking along Lake Michigan.
He's come up with some of his best ideas, he says, sitting
in the park or while welding auto bumpers into sculpture
in his garage. The one place he says he doesn't get much
thinking done is in his office, so he only spends enough
time there to pass along his ideas to his subordinates.

"Tinkham Veale II, chairman of Alco Standard Corporation," says the *Journal* piece, "does his work in an old
stable in his two-hundred-acre estate in Fates Mills,
Ohio," some four hundred miles from Alco's headquarters. Outside his office is a picturesque complex of old
white frame buildings, terraced lawns, manicured gardens, greenhouses, stables and pastures for Mr. Veale's
horses. His day begins at 6:30 A.M. when he spends an
hour wandering around the estate, "to get the cobwebs

out." Running his office from home allows him to "continue business meetings well into the night" if the need arises.

Philadelphia public relations man Philip Bucci moves aboard his fifty-foot yacht from June through October and runs his office from Chesapeake Bay. "I can avoid the anxieties and tensions of the usual office routine. Without question, it's helped my work a lot." There's another motive for Philip Bucci's living aboard. "So many guys die of heart attacks in my business that I felt this was really a necessary thing I had to do."

Perhaps there *is* something real and reasonable in wanting to work the hours when you produce your best ideas. Maybe there is something to Arkansas-Louisiana Gas Co. president W. R. Stephen's belief that working with your hands helps you to work with your mind. Perhaps Tinkham Veale II, who begins the day wandering about his estate, and Philip Bucci, who looks up from his typewriter to gaze at the waters of the Chesapeake Bay, would agree with less affluent dropouts who say they find in nature a daily source of renewal.

According to every executive and management consultant we talked to, the problem isn't one of too much freedom, but of too little. Business consultant Anthony Jay says that too few executives have the freedoms that really matter.

Political freedom: executives are often inhibited from campaigning for political office, or a political party, because their employer is fearful of customer or community antagonisms.

Freedom to publish: many executives cannot write newspaper or magazine articles without clearing them with the corporation.

Freedom of speech: if executives gave their subordinates or the press details of higher management incompetence, they would likely be fired.

According to *U. S. News and World Report*'s account of a study conducted by the Life Extension Institute of New York, which conducts health examinations for about 35,-000 businessmen a year, "today's manager drinks more at lunch, worries more about his decisions, has more trouble getting to sleep and is more dissatisfied with the progress he is making than he was a dozen years ago."

While a drink at lunch is rarely prohibited, and may even be encouraged at business luncheons, practically no corporations encourage employees and officers to work during their "best" hours, unless those hours happen to be between 9 A.M. and 5 P.M., nor would they permit vice presidents, salesmen and accountants to work in blue jeans and tennis shoes. Neither do most corporations allow executives to live outside the boundaries of narrow limits of acceptable behavior.

What most managers envy is not the two-hundred-acre estate or the fifty-foot yacht, but the right to work one's best hours, to be close to nature, free of ritual and the responsibility to live up to an image. What many of these executives are beginning to realize is that they don't have to fight their way to the top to gain control of their own lives. All they have to do is walk out the office door.

"If these guys want out so bad," asked the industrial relations vice president of a major corporation, "what's keeping them?" A good question. The answer lies with the fact that many men who stay in year after year don't know why they do it. Once they learn what's been driving them (one man called it, The Four Horsemen of Status, Security, Success and Solvency), they often quit.

"What happens to us," says Chevy Chase, Maryland, psychiatrist (and former National Institute of Mental Health researcher) Dr. Arden A. Flint, "is that we've been conditioned to work for symbols, the empty calories of emotional fulfillment, instead of learning to discover our own values. Like men on a vitamin-deficient diet, we keep on wanting 'more' because our real needs aren't being met."

We learn in school to work for straight "A" report cards and to make the team. In college, many of today's achievers strained to make the "best" fraternities and to date the best-looking girls. "It's no surprise then," adds psychiatrist Flint, "that men end up working for titles and possessions and status; society's *symbols* of success, instead of the real thing, which for some might be good family relationships or living a particular life style."

Scores of achievers we talked with in researching this book, men who were getting ahead in the rat race, say the real barrier facing them in getting out was not so much a problem of finding work, cutting down expenses, or retraining for a new career. It was the step-by-step process of rejecting corporate values and replacing them, one by one, with their own.

2

The Burdens of Corporate Life

Like any other businessman, Richard Covington reaches out to turn off his alarm clock every morning a little earlier then he'd like to, and like any other businessman he shuffles into the bathroom to begin the daily ritual of shaving and dressing for work.

Like any other businessman he downs a quick breakfast, says, "See you later, kids," and gives his wife a fleeting kiss on his way out the door.

And like any other businessman, Richard Covington puts down his briefcase on the seat beside him, and eases his car back down his driveway into the street to join the mainstream of other men bound for the city for another day at the office.

But, unlike other businessmen, Richard Covington doesn't have a job. He has been "merged out," and at this writing hasn't been employed for more than three months. For a man making nearly $50,000 a year, losing his job was a trauma that all but immobilized him. He still hasn't found the strength to tell anyone but his wife that he's unemployed.

The name we use here isn't his own, but Richard Covington's story is real. "Like a lot of other guys my age," he told me as we sat together on the mezzanine of a plush downtown hotel where he sometimes used to have lunch in better days, "I was brought up to believe the way you earned your balls in the world was to get ahead, and I put an awful lot into that—getting ahead and earning my balls in business.

"After I got out of Princeton right after the war, I went with one of the electrical appliance manufacturers in sales. Television was just coming in then and I figured that if I'd just work hard and do my job the tide would carry me along. I did pretty well and was offered a bigger job with a competitor, took it for six years, and then decided to try my wings as a manufacturer's representative.

"I did well enough. I was making around $30,000 which wasn't bad in 1961, but I found I was missing some of the things that go with being a corporation executive. I guess you could say I'm a corporate man. I enjoyed the office and the reserved parking place, and the club memberships and all the rest of it. I realize now that that's what I worked for as much as for the money, so when one of the companies I represented offered me their sales vice-presidency, I grabbed it.

"I'd been around long enough to know that when the company was bought out it was all over for me there, but I couldn't resign. I kept coming in like nothing happened and they finally had to give me the word. The first month I couldn't even tell my wife. Fortunately, I received a pretty fair severance check so I carefully put the exact amount of my former pay in the bank on the regular deposit day, and my ex-secretary covered for me when my wife called."

Richard Covington hasn't told his children yet that there's no job to go to, and though he talks about it with his wife, he can't bring himself to mention his plight to his friends or the few neighbors he's come to know during the six years he's lived in his $60,000 home.

"I have a couple of job possibilities now," he told me, "but I'll never make it like I did before." He hopes one of his out-of-town jobs comes through soon, though, so he can "just quietly move away from this town."

"I let it creep up on me," he said as we stood on the sidewalk outside the hotel's front door. "I wanted the things that went with my job so much that I *became* my job, and when the job was gone there wasn't anything left."

Something *was* left, of course, but at that point in Richard Covington's life, he was still captive to one of the classic illusions of the corporate world—that the job is the measure of the man, rather than the other way around.

How do women fare in the corporate life? Do they share in the general malaise reported by their male colleagues? Why are there so few stories of women dropouts from the corporate world? Will the pattern be changing?

Margaret Hennig, a Visiting Associate Professor at Harvard's Graduate School of Business Administration, has a quick answer to the last question. "Yes, the pattern *will* be changing. And for the better, where women are concerned. It really has nowhere else to go, given the distortions of women's participation in the labor force during the past ten years. Since women still have only about fifteen percent of 'managerial' jobs, only four percent at the top of the skill, status, and income ladder, it's no wonder that few of them are ready to bite the hand that has been gracious enough to feed them. Most very successful women executives, in fact, are delighted to be where they are, and wouldn't think of complaining about the pressures of the system. Indeed, many of them take considerable pride in their ability to master those pressures, and often have a tendency to measure their own achievement against what they view as the failure of other women to match their brilliance and tough-mindedness."

Professor Hennig wrote to fifty top women executives in the fall of 1972, chosen at random from *Fortune Magazine*'s five hundred top corporations. She asked them to talk briefly about what they would "most like to tell (Professor Hennig's) seminar students about women in industry and management."

The replies were uniformly positive, in the sense that the women respondents affirmed in general terms the opportunities for women in industry, and in virtually no case admitted that women with ability and gumption were thwarted in reaching the highest echelons of executive power.

One vice president of a major food producer, for example, writes: "Women today have outstanding opportunities available to them in business and industry. Unfortunately, too few women are prepared to assume these responsibilities. . . . I find that many young women . . . do not have the driving ambition which helps speed many men to the top."

Another industry vice president sent a detailed *curriculum vitae,* a copy of a speech she'd given on "The Woman's Place in International Business," and the interesting remark that, "I would say [the] most important [qualification for a woman to suceed in business] is tremendous flexibility, a sense of humor, a certain amount of humility because for many men a woman still has to 'prove' herself."

Professor Hennig thinks these sentiments are understandable, and even well-intentioned, but also dated. "It won't be long," she says, "before women executives stop thinking of themselves as blessed curiosities in a man's world, and start talking as if their role in the business world were essentially androgynous—based on what they can do, and how well, and how much of the organizational life they're willing to put up with in order to share in its benefits."

One respondent who sensed the meaning of that shift, the director of "Retail Systems Support" for a large business machines manufacturer, wrote: "If only someone had organized a course for me in 'The Practical Aspects of Life as a Woman Executive'—preparation for such occasions as when one of your new managers comes into your office, closes the door behind him, sits resolutely in a chair before you, and says 'You and I are going to have a talk. I'm not sure I'm comfortable working for a woman.' Well, one learns to improvise and to respond creatively and diplomatically. And after a while it becomes known that one is a good manager, who happens to be a woman.

". . . Anyone who is in a management position knows that 85 percent of your time is spent dealing with people —your peers, the people you report to, and most importantly, the people who report to you. It is this last group to which there must be the strongest commitment. The people who work for you must be directed, motivated, moved to produce, and helped to grow. If they succeed, you succeed. But not until they regard you first as a professional and a manager, and second as a woman, can you be effective."

The most obvious explanation, however, of why so few women executives at the upper levels declare themselves out of the ratrace, is that very few of such women have families dependent upon them for economic support—and they are under no pressure, therefore, to remain in jobs that seem repressive or stultifying because there is no obvious alternative source of income. Either such women have husbands who are *also* quite successful in business ("Many high-salaried women have husbands who are even more high-salaried," says Professor Hennig), or they have no husband at all, and are fully involved in the business of business. Increasingly, however, women who are heads of households or the major wage carrier are assuming positions of managerial leadership.

At the lower and middle levels of the corporate work force, however, many young women are going through precisely the same fits of uneasiness experienced by their male counterparts. Here is Mary Jo French, for example, talking to a reporter from *Cosmopolitan* magazine: "It was exciting to be a copywriter at first—pulling in hundreds of dollars a week and bonuses that equalled another half-year's pay, just for writing about artichokes or hair dryers. But I reached a psychological point after two years where I wanted *out*. The money couldn't assuage my boredom."

Mary Jo French now runs a boutique in Los Angeles, where she designs her own clothes. She has had better luck, so far, than thirty-four-year-old Liz Long, who quit her high-paid job as head librarian at a large advertising agency after a disconcerting bout with a late movie. "One night I saw the film *Desk Set* on TV . . . and when I saw the resemblance to my own office setup with its rows of human computers, I decided to quit the very next day . . . I was making a fantastic salary, had traveled to Europe, the Caribbean, California several times, lived in a lovely apartment, and really didn't know what to do with my money *next.* As a result my paycheck meant less and less to me, but the constant pressure at work was making me more and more unhappy.

"Eventually I found a job that offered decent pay, little responsibility, and the short hours I needed to write my novel . . . what I really wanted to do. No, none of my writing has been published yet, but if success is being happy, I've arrived."

At twenty-nine, Anita Gross had reached the upper levels of a profession with no more than a couple of dozen truly prospering examplars—and no more than forty or fifty full-time practitioners at all. She was a New York literary agent, the number two nameplate in a small office headed by Lynn Nesbit, an aggressive and dynamic young woman still in her thirties who, like Anita, came out of the backwoods of Ohio, started out as a secretary, and soon outstripped all but a handful of the other professionals in her field. In January, 1973, Anita Gross was making more than $15,000 a year (compared to the $80 a week she got from McGraw-Hill, where she started as a secretary in the spring of 1965). But in early March, she left the agent business, prepared to leave New York, and began feeling like her own person for the first time in years.

"I don't have a specific plan," she says, "though I want

to move to San Francisco and catch my breath for a while. I don't kid myself that the move is a solution to the problems I've felt about my life for the past couple of years, but I *do* know I've got to get out of this life, and the pressures that come with it.

"It's been months since I've had the chance to read a book for pleasure, something I used to enjoy. And the homework in this job is so perpetual, and so demanding, that I'd find myself sitting at home, hacking away at it, too tired to spend time with the man in my life.

"It's funny, you know, when I thought about giving up this job, which I've loved, I realized how frightened I was that I wouldn't be able to find something as worthwhile on the West Coast. Are they going to make me a secretary again, is what I kept asking myself. Women lack confidence, I think, that they really have carved out a place for themselves, no matter how good they are. I hope that changes."

It may seem perverse, but the conclusion is unavoidable: when significant numbers of highly placed women executives start breaking away from the confinement of corporation life, we may assume that the sex-based distortions of the labor force have largely been corrected. At that point, women will no longer be forced to console themselves with the private satisfaction that at least they have succeeded where other women fail, and they will be looking toward other satisfactions, the sense of tapping that larger potential for direct human involvement, the temptations of other callings. It is possible, of course, that American industry, as discussed in a later chapter of this book, will find ways to preserve and give expression to the better instincts of productive executives. And if recent history has any meaning, these developments are likely to take into account the accelerating influx of highly skilled, highly motivated women into the middle and upper ranks of the business world. Whether that genuinely brave new world will include many women as family breadwinners remains to be seen. If that should come to pass, the whole pattern of corporate angst, as Professor Hennig suggests, will be radically changed indeed.

For nearly two decades, social psychologist Dr. Charles Seashore has worked intimately with top-level management in many of America's largest manufacturing firms, banks, utilities and government agencies. Prior to establishing his own consulting firm in Washington, D. C., he served with National Training Laboratories, originators of "T-groups," sensitivity programs for high-level corporate officials, as trainer-director of research and professional development.

He has seen the price men pay for membership in the corporate society life. "To begin with, men in the corporate structure are unaware, most of the time, of the degree to which their goals are set for them. By being involved in a large corporation they have certain things determined for them as life goals, and certain other things, outside interests, for example, which are not readily obtainable because they're not supported by the organization. They're trapped into certain goals and trapped out of others.

"For example, the notions as to what progress in growth and status is, are by and large organizationally determined. If you have been around an organization long enough, you get tied to the idea of working for a bigger office or whatever. After a year or so you lose touch with the fact that those things have, in fact, become very important to you. Then you start noticing how big offices are, and desks, and the whole set-up. By and large, these are not very sufficient things for human development.

"I was working with a large organization that provides a good example of how ideas can be shaped just by daily contact with the physical structure of the corporation. This organization installed potted plants in the offices of its executives, and discovered that the plants were dying, through neglect or whatever, at an alarmingly high rate. So the company decided to replace real plants with plastic imitations, in all middle and upper-management offices.

"The initial reaction was one of revulsion, 'Look at that miserable plastic plant: I'd rather have my office bare than have one of those.' But within six months, the same executives were chiefly concerned with the *size* of the plant in their office—and were zealous in comparing their plastic shrubbery with that installed in the offices of everyone at their management level."

"I think," says Dr. Seashore, "that business 'friendships' for personal advantage are a very common thing. People are invited into the home, weekend trips are shared, and activities which otherwise might be enjoyable are diluted by the requirement to cultivate superiors, customers, and at the highest level, even competitors."

Former executives who recall these pressures complain of the feeling of always being on stage, and having almost every thought they expressed censored by a corporate conscience implanted within the brain. "Every time I opened my mouth," said one former Ford Motor Company V. P., "I had to think like a politician running for reelection. I had the realization that every word I said, in the office or out, could be taken and dissected for hidden meanings, including possible shifting shades of loyalty to my company or to corporate ethic generally. I had to plan my escape with stealth and mis-direction, aware that, if discovered before I was ready to make the break, I could be shot as a deserter."

According to Dr. Seashore, life in the corporation structure often traps men through its basic use of their time. "Their whole daily, weekly, monthly and yearly calendar gets set for them in a way they may not have perceived. If you can only say which two weeks of the year you want to take your vacation, that's not a very significant part of a year, and it's not a very significant choice.

"Right up to the top vice-presidential level, time demands the organization have priority in one's life. It's always possible at any moment that the corporate time press will take precedence in one's life. There are only a few instances, like hospitalization or family death, where personal time needs may surmount corporate time needs.

"If the president of the company calls on Friday night and says, 'I want you to go to California,' and your child wants to learn how to ride her new two-wheeler on Saturday, it's hardly acceptable to say, 'I can't go to California, I want to teach my child how to ride her bicycle.' In other words, personal things become postponable.

"Many families don't fully experience these conflicts. Corporate men teach their wives, and children soon learn, that the organization has priority in their lives.

"Perhaps one of the worst things about many organizations," concludes Dr. Seashore, "is that you have relatively few supports for getting out of that organization, especially if you are a valuable person. The people around you start planning your life and your career without even talking with you about it. They start looking at you as someone who can be moved into one slot or another tomorrow or in a few years."

Barton Knapp and Marta Vago work with some of the problems that men bring home from the office, not in their briefcases, but in their bodies and in their heads. Bart and Marta are codirectors of Laurel Institute in Philadelphia, a family counseling and psychology center. Dr. Knapp has his Ph.D. in psychology from the University of Syracuse; Marta Vago, her master's in social work from Temple University.

Dr. Knapp and Miss Vago say that when it comes to looking at some of the penalties men and their families pay for being caught up in the rat race, being treated like a commodity is one of the worst, "because when you do this to an individual what happens is that he tends to treat others like commodities. If a man comes to feel that he is being thought of as an object for manipulation—to be moved here or there at the company's convenience without consideration for his interests or home life, then you can probably expect him to treat others like commodities, like objects for manipulation.

"If you think about the implication of this upon family life, marital relations, children, communities, friendships and so on, you begin to see that when a man is caught up in the rat race, everybody around him is caught up in the rat race.

"In terms of some of the other prices that families pay,

it is our impression that there's just so much energy a person has; an individual is not a bottomless well that never runs dry. If a man only sees his family when he's hassled, or when he'd really like some peace and quiet away from people, it is going to have a tremendous effect on the quality of family life.

"If the children or his wife never see him relaxed, or rested or just 'being,' then every contact this person has with his family is going to have an element of strain in it. We think the quality of serenity that a man can bring to his wife and children is one of the most crucial elements of family life.

"The whole family really gets caught up in the rat race, with mothers wanting their children to be exposed to the 'good things in life,' and shuttling them to and from dancing lessons, Brownies, Girl Scouts, Boy Scouts, and what-have-you, so that the family is always in a state of tension, trying to keep up, trying just to keep even and not drown in all the appurtenances of a successful life."

Ron Kahn, former executive recruiter, was a man who had all the appurtenances of success and lived an empty life. His $35,000 a year income bought him a decent home and thirty-foot boat to play with on weekends, but his concentration on achieving the ends, by any means at all, "cost me the lighter side of my life and blew my marriage."

Ron Kahn was "born hustling" and took to "head-hunting" as the newest in a long line of hustles that began with high-pressure magazine subscription sales and included selling hearing aids to senior citizens touted into his shop for "free hearing-aid clinics" and to have their hearing aids "winterized—Yeah, *winterized*. It was unbelievable the things we'd do, like putting a small drop of oil on the inside of their hearing aids to foul up the works.

"In those days, before I got out," continues Kahn, "when I met someone, I was only concerned with what could I use him for, what could I do with him, what does he want from me; what sort of threat is he to me; this was my way of meeting people. I viewed people as potential enemies.

"Like a lot of people I wasn't really getting satisfaction out of what the money could buy me. I was a guy who never saw a tree; I never saw a simple tree before, and I never heard a bird. I never knew they were out there making music."

During his two "headhunting" years, Ron Kahn built up a national following among corporations who knew he could be counted on to deliver. He would tell clients, "You know what we do; we're pirates. We're going to get information from you about your competition and you're going to tell us who's giving you the most trouble and I'm going to take their key person and give him to you.

"They always went into long dissertations about how ethical they were and how they couldn't become involved in anything like that sort of thing—and how important it was that nobody knew they were involved. Then they would hire us and pay our fee."

He investigated his quarry and would find out what his income was, how large a mortgage he carried, how many children he had, how stable his situation was, and whether he had already refused any offers to move, before he called his prospect on the phone. "We appealed to his ego or his greed or whatever it took to get him. We disrupted his life and came between the husband and wife in cases where she was against the move.

"We'd fly to his home and have a conversation with the husband and wife and tell her what a selfish woman she was for holding him back; that he had sacrificed for her and now she was holding him back. We were trying to make her hysterical so she'd start crying and all she could say was that she just didn't want him to go. If we had a really difficult time recruiting a man we'd manage to get him fired. After that we didn't have a difficult time recruiting him."

Ron Kahn was becoming a success, but he was beginning to have problems with his conscience. "I got to the point where I couldn't function. I could no longer stand what I was doing to people; the divorces, people's careers completely ruined, men's loss of financial security and companies that went down the drain because we took their entire management teams, piece by piece—things like that.

"I was in a place with myself where my pleasures weren't even pleasures. I was a good poker player and I realized I wasn't there to play poker; I was there to grind money from the people I was playing with. It was the kind of poker where, if you open your mouth, you have a problem. The only time you said anything was to bet. No conversation. No enjoyment.

"My boss knew something was troubling me. I guess I didn't disguise it. Anyway, one day he handed me a note telling me to go to a certain group encounter he knew of. After that encounter I began to get in touch with myself, and before long was able to say 'goodbye' to headhunting."

Thirty-six-year-old advertising man Bruce Hiptak never quite lost himself to the organization. He'd worked

in the advertising department of Southern Bell, "learning the yellow pages," moved up to better pay at Young
& Rubicam advertising agency, and back into the yellow
pages again, the last time for General Telephone and
Electronics, "GT&E," as he calls it.

For Bruce Hiptak it was the *Playboy* life all the way.
"The only thing I had time for in those days was to make
money and to spend it, which was my total endeavor. I
kept telling myself that if I could only make a little more
money, things would be better. I was trying to do things
that would make me happy, such as traveling with female
companions, typical dates of a hundred dollars, going on
really outrageously expensive weekends—things like
that.

"I had a couple of cars, plus a sports car, the whole,
whole deal. But none of this stuff gave me any happiness
really. What surprised me when I began to see it was that
I could be so unhappy when, by society's standards, I had
it made. I was a good catch, from the standpoint of a girl,
and many times I was under pressure to get married.

"At the time I was going up the ladder I was drinking
and getting pains in my stomach. There were certainly a
lot of gratifications in a good advertising campaign and
every once in a while, people I worked with would agree
that I had done a good job and when those rare moments
came along it was really great.

"When I was in the business I was good, really good.
Therefore, I was allowed to say things and express myself occasionally. But whenever things got a little bit
down they used to take all those things I had said, in
meetings and so on, and really put on the pressure. And
I was traveling all the time, wherever there was a yellow
pages promotion.

"One day I started looking around and saw that some people were happy, and they weren't people with the money I had. The travel, being hassled by GT&E, and not getting anything out of it—finally one day I just decided I wasn't going to take it. So I did what a typically frustrated person does. I just got out. Then when I had gotten out I had this terrific gnawing to get back in. That really surprised me.

"My income went from good to zero and I drove a boat around to make a little money. I was trying to find myself. All of a sudden I had time to communicate with people. This I hadn't been able to do before because I was too bound up in my little world to speak to or get to know anyone.

"All along I'd been getting favorable words from my parents, my whole family, and everything I did was O.K. When I got out, their reaction was that I just threw everything away: 'How can you do this? How can you throw away your education? How can you, after all we've done?' But who do you respond to, them or you?"

If it hadn't been for the family pressure to become a professional in one way or another, Myron Travis "Mike" Weiner might never have become a psychologist. "I think I might have been a farmer, believe it or not. Part of my background was weekends in the country outside New York City. During the summer we'd live there full time and my father would commute. So I sort of grew up in the country; I dug it.

"During my clinical practice period in Atlanta I was pretty much a straight therapist; Sullivanian and Rogerian, which was the approach of my supervisor in graduate school. I finished my Ph.D. in psychology at the University of Texas when I was thirty-four.

"School, to me, was really rotten. I liked the idea of

getting a Ph.D.; you know, it's nice to be called 'doctor,' but I doubt seriously that even 10 percent of my education was related to the goal I was seeking.

"I had to have working papers to be able to get a license to practice, and yet practically none of the education was relevant to what I wanted to do. Of course I believed I was going through all this so I could help people, but somewhere along the way I lost track of what I was doing, or why. It wasn't until fifteen years later that I felt I was living the kind of life I really wanted to live. That's a lot of years down the drain.

"The last year I operated the office I had a $40,000 house with two fireplaces, three bathrooms. Also, a swimming pool in the back yard, which I could ill afford. My wife was interested in having all these things, and I was too, of course, but while I was getting in touch with different values of my own, we grew apart. Now I am divorced. . . ."

Today Mike Weiner and Bruce Hiptak are partners in the Om Shop, located in the Coconut Grove section of Miami, Florida. Mike's former hobby of jewelry making and Bruce's new-found interest in leather and other crafts are providing them both with a far more comfortable living than their previous high incomes were ever able to give them.

There are other men who find some signs too painful to read at all. John Wood, former aerospace engineer who got out just before defense cutbacks decimated aircraft industry payrolls, told me this story one day when we were talking in his San Diego, California, living room: "In our company, we were always under a lot of pressure, job insecurities, because the nature of our business was that on almost every big contract we had to bid against other aerospace companies.

"We never knew, as we approached the end of a contract, whether or not the company would get a new one to keep us working. So there was this constant threat of losing your job; plus every project being a crash project and never having enough people to do the job because the company had to keep certain costs down to get the contract. Tremendous pressures.

"Well, one of the things we used to do when someone would get sick—having a heart attack was frequent—was that the rest of the guys, his fellow workers, would all sit around and try to figure out why he had had it and try to justify it. In other words, it wasn't because of the pressures or the schedules or the frustrations that the guy was getting from his boss—or anything to do with the job at all.

"It was always because the guy was overweight, or because he smoked too much and didn't stop when the doctor told him to. Any reason we could come up with, which took some doing with an underweight guy who didn't smoke, would be advanced by his coworkers to explain why he deserved having a heart attack and they wouldn't.

"I think part of it was our own fear, not being able to face that we were all in the same place as far as having a heart attack was concerned."

When laid-off aerospace engineers and scientists began to glut the job market in 1970, the state of California hired John Wood to conduct workshops for unemployed men in how to find new jobs. Some of the things he learned from working with hundreds of men were that, "what they needed most was to find out who they were and what they were doing with their lives. In a way they were glad they were out and that it had all happened because they would never have quit on their own. But they still operated on the old habit patterns of looking for chances of promotion, high pay, and offices and all that. So they're free on the one hand, and yet it's frightening on the other."

In working with California's unemployed aerospace engineers, John Wood learned what many company presidents have yet to discover; that the numbers of men who are getting out voluntarily are only the part of the iceberg that appears above the surface. "For every man who gets out of the rat race," assert New York organizational development consultants Dr. William Gellerman and Bradley Brewer, "there are many who are killing large and small pieces of themselves and who are not performing up to their potential.

"There are plenty of men not performing as well as they can because of a gap between what they perceive the company wants from them and what they are prepared to give. That gap is painful and a fellow can deal with it in a number of ways. He might want to tell the company how he feels about its invasion of his life, or pressures to compromise his ethics and so on, but he usually has the idea that the company will come down hard on him and that he'd be committing career suicide. So he'll probably try to live with it and suffer and eat his insides out. The only way these men can perform at their potential is to close the value gap between what they want to give, and what the corporation wants them to give.

"The guy who suffers with a value gap pays a certain price for staying on. He can pay the price of finding it harder and harder to come to work in the morning, by becoming an alcoholic, or taking up with his secretary to try to forget it all. Some guys go crazy, some guys end up on dope. It can take a lot of forms, but one thing that happens is that they, consciously or unconsciously, do various kinds of attack things on themselves. I know one guy who's making money hand over fist and he's impotent and wonders why. I don't wonder why.

"Beyond making it harder to close the value gap, the authoritarian management mode followed by many corporations today makes it very difficult for good men to make the contribution they need to make in order to be happy. All too often what men may see as being in the best interests of the company is not what the company perceives as its best interests. These guy may be wrong, or the boss might value their inputs, but too often the environment does not encourage these risks and, in many cases, when a group is trying to solve a problem, the man says what he feels he's expected to say, just to play it safe.

"The problem is that in an authority-based system where the general waits to kill the messenger who brings the bad news, a fellow is not encouraged to raise problems. He's possibly well advised to keep his observations to himself because it's not going to enhance his reputation in an organization that likes to think of its waters as smooth. If he identifies a problem that's staring them right in the face, he's likely to get credit for being a trouble-maker.

"When a guy feels he's in this kind of situation, he's usually tempted to get out and often he does, either by quitting or by setting himself up to be squeezed out. It's just a different mechanism for walking out—they walk out forwards or backwards, but they're still out—and probably happier."

But Bill Gellerman and Brad Brewer think there may

be another avenue for men to take before walking off the job. "What if, instead of just saying, 'Fuck you,' to the company, a man says, 'Well, there are different ways of saying those two words and there are different ways to walk out, so long as I've decided that I'm getting out anyway, I might as well see how honest I can be and what changes I can make for the better because I don't have that much to risk.'

"He could say, in effect, 'I don't know how long I'm going to last in this place, but if the time comes when I'm no longer around I would like you to be haunted by the voice of someone who said, "Jesus, gentlemen, one day we're just going to have to do the right thing and I think this is the right thing and I don't think it will kill us to do it. I can't blackjack anybody into agreement with me and if this is seen as some kind of sabotage then I'll have to go. I'd like to stay around and make my input, but I don't want to be any other way, because there's no other way that I want to define myself." ' "

Whether a man decides to get out of the corporation walking forward or backward, or decides to take the risk of exile, he may feel that the material things his position provides for his family can be replaced by more basic nonmaterial things, such as being a better father and husband. But there is little acceptance in the corporate world of the man who places nonmaterial goals above material ones.

3

Five Who Got Out

Larry Murphy, Bill Neely, Ralph Graham, David Youland, and Bob Cromey are five among the scores of people we interviewed who broke out. Like the others they
use their time as they choose, devote their energies to
things that interest them, and are free of roles which had
kept them from being themselves.

Like the others, they aren't "supermen" who have succeeded where lesser individuals are bound to fail. They
share their strengths and weaknesses with the rest of us.
They and the many others whose experiences contribute
to this book, have three basic circumstances in common:

None had significant savings to fall back on should
things not work out.

None had an outside income. When their salaries
stopped, their incomes ended. (There are plenty of
wealthy "dropouts," but none were included in this vol-
ume.)

None had a rich relative standing in the wings to help
them pick up the pieces if they fell.

There are a number of other distinguishing character-
istics among the men and women I met who were successful in breaking out:

They traded the symbols of success and pleasure—
clubs, status homes and cars, notoriety and private
offices—for their own kinds of wealth: time for families
to be together, creation of jobs free of any one boss, and
greater intimacy with nature, not as a refuge, but as a
source.

There seems to be a natural freedom in their lives
from the many roles that society assigns to men and
women, parents and children, bosses and employees and
teachers and the taught. Members of families that have
broken out say they're now freer to learn from each
other, more able to accept love and capable of encoun-
tering new people in their lives less limited by precon-
ceptions that formerly colored the experience of meeting.

They tend to form friendships in which they share a
wider range of emotions and activities. There is more
talking and listening to music and "doing nothing" together. There is more sharing of jobs to be done instead
of restricting contacts to recreational activities. I saw
more evidence of anger and impatience—and more expression of love and affection than I see among others.

People who have broken out seem to deal with the way
things *are,* more than they lament the way things *should*
be. If they can do something to put a situation right they
do it. If they can't they don't bewail the circumstance.

Their needs seem simple. Like the girl in a famous
soap commercial, they've "gone back to basics." Their
possessions are usually fewer than before and they are
"worth less" than in their former lives. Free of what they

call "symbolic possessions and pleasures," their worldly goods exist to meet real needs rather than make up for living a dull life, or lack of self-esteem, or recognition, or love or power.

They live in what they like to call "the here and now." Beyond putting something aside for real emergencies, they devote little effort and make few sacrifices toward living that is to be put off until some time in the future. There are few plans for retirement or for "after the children are grown."

Holidays and anniversaries, clocks and calendars, mean less than when they were keeping step with society. New Year's Day may be the occasion for a hard day's work—if there's work to be done. Wedding dates and birthdays may be lived through with scarcely a ripple; yet feasts may be celebrated for themselves or a gift given just for the giving of a gift. Shrimp cocktail might be served for breakfast or a full meal cooked for someone when he or she wakes up hungry in the middle of the night.

People who have left the rat race behind seem not to be looking for hidden or true meanings of life. If they can be said to be asking any philosophical question in forming their response to the choices that daily confront them, it seems less to be a matter of "Why?" than "Why not?"

There is one more thing. In breaking out almost all had help. For some it was the example of intimate friends whose own breaking free they could experience on a "gut" level that taught them something about themselves.

For the most part though, breaking out came gradually through working with a psychiatrist or psychologist or through participation in some kind of growth experience such as Primal Therapy, Gestalt Therapy, encounter, sensitivity training or corporate sponsored "T-Group" programs.

But the differences among successful escapees are as great as the similarities. Some gave up religion, others found it. Some changed their work, others changed only its direction. Some live on far less money than before, but for many, incomes are higher. Some moved across the country, others moved little more than across the street.

There were divorces, but apparently with relatively little pain because changes seem to have come about through mutual recognition of real needs and disparities in the lives of some husbands and wives. Other couples with many years together say that only since breaking out have they been really close.

Their pasts are as diverse as their todays. Some came from wealthy backgrounds and permanently severed family and financial ties in leaving family businesses. Others supported themselves even as children and had as early goals only the acquisition of money and power.

Some became teachers. Others gave it up. Some went back to school for advanced degrees, others in learned professions began working with their hands.

Many were young when they took the first steps toward changing their lives. Others had considerable years invested in corporate retirement programs when they decided their futures, even their tomorrows, were too valuable to sell for a monthly annuity check.

The five families which make up the following few chapters are fairly representative of the main body of people we met and interviewed for this book. Three of the five have young children. One husband and wife, each previously married, have no children of their own living with them. One man is divorced, has not remarried, and supports his children.

Three were in what is loosely called "business." One was an airline pilot and one was a minister. All are gainfully employed and living off of earned income. One of the four wives works with her husband. One works at a separate job and two don't work.

Although one can find examples at either end of the bell curve, the experiences of the Bill Neely, Larry Murphy, Ralph Graham, David Youland families, and of Bob Cromey, are fairly typical, I think, of those who broke out.

4

Larry Murphy: From Airline Pilot to Potter

For nearly eleven years, Larry Murphy enjoyed status and prosperity as a highly trained expert in one of the most demanding professions the American system has to offer a young man. As a Navy pilot he flew sleek A-4 Skyhawk jet fighter-bombers from the deck of the carrier Ranger in the Pacific, often making night landings on a pitching deck in weather that would have closed commercial airports to arriving traffic.

For four years following his naval service, he flew giant Boeing 707 airliners for Pan American World Airways over some of the same Pacific waters he had seen from the cockpit of a single-engine Navy jet. His everyday uniform included a white shirt, black tie, trousers and jacket with gold stripes.

Today Larry Murphy wears faded blue jeans, sandals, and denim work shirts. People buy his pots and plates and vases and cups in San Francisco's Ghirardelli Square, as well as in art shows around the state of California.

For much of his adult life, Larry Murphy collected labels for himself. They were: athlete, Navy jet pilot, Central Intelligence Agency mercenary, and airline pilot. He needed, he says, to be liked and respected. Today, if he thinks about labels at all, he'd tell you that the label "potter" is the most comfortable one he's ever worn.

"When I was in parochial school," he says, "I got the idea that in order to be accepted by my peers and those in authority I had to show that I could *produce*. Just being Larry Murphy wasn't enough. Though my folks accepted me just because I was me, I kept getting the message from outside that I had to have a front, a sign, to tell the world I was worthwhile.

"In high school I'd always wanted to be an athlete, because that's where the recognition was, a letter for your sweater and all, but I was never good enough at sports. I think I wasn't good enough because I didn't want it bad enough. I didn't want to play ball that much. I wanted to be an *athlete*, to be *known* as an *athlete*, but I didn't want to play football or basketball or any of the other sports that badly.

"When I graduated from college I had no idea what I wanted to do. I remember I was walking through the halls one day and the Navy recruiter was there. He had a big poster with a picture of a guy in his flight suit with his flying helmet under his arm standing by the nose of a jet. I thought, 'Wow, that's what I'll do.' If they'd told me I couldn't be a jet pilot, that I'd have to fly multi-engine, it wouldn't have meant anything to me.

"I'd never been good enough for the varsity, but now by God, I was going to do something that would give me *machismo*. If I couldn't do it on a basketball court, then I'd do it in the cockpit of an airplane.

"The day after I got my wings, I thought I was more

worthwhile than I'd been the day before. It was like getting an 'A' on your report card, or a letter for your
sweater if you're an athlete—when the world has taught
you you aren't anything until you have something to
show people to prove that you are.

"Looking back, I'm surprised I wasn't more of a maverick in the Navy, but I believed in the Navy way. There
was something intangible about it though, that wasn't
right, that I couldn't explain. I wasn't confronting the
system, I was part of it and never questioned it.

"You're taught not to question that stuff, like the
Church, the government, school administration, and the
squadron commander. Your parents are right because
they're your parents. A teacher is right, a cop is right,
authority is right. It's a magnificent tool for control.

"Once the squadron executive officer was putting on
a skit that included a scene about taking a hot bath in
Japan and I was supposed to appear on stage as the guy
taking the bath. The executive officer said I was going to
do it and I said I wasn't going to do it and that he could
get someone else. He said, 'You're junior man in the
squadron and you're going to do it. . . . If you don't
you're going to find yourself in a hell of a lot of trouble.'

"I didn't do the part, and I didn't get in a lot of trouble. The squadron exec was probably making points and
everybody else up there was probably doing it to make
points, and maybe the C. O. and other brass were there
watching it because it was expected of them. It wouldn't
surprise me. There was an awful lot of show like that in
the Navy."

There were rewards and grades and lists on the bulle-
tin board. It's hard to deal with the reality of who you are
with all that kid stuff going on. It might be good for the
Navy, but it wasn't good for *me*.

"When these things started happening, I felt I had to get out, so I applied to the Peace Corps and was accepted for assignment to Bolivia as soon as I got my discharge. I went to the Peace Corps offices in Washington and asked if someone could tell me anything about my assignment.

"Well, when I got there nobody knew who I was, even though I had sent a letter telling them I was coming. Nobody could tell me anything about anything, even when I could expect to start. So I went to the Central Intelligence Agency and asked them if they were looking for guys who were about to get out of the Navy and they said, 'Possibly. Fill out this application.' When I got out of the Navy I still hadn't heard from them, because there was a sixteen-month clearance process.

"I went to San Francisco State College and got a teaching credential and met Rose, who was working as a fashion copywriter for a department store. We got married and I went to work for Kaiser Steel in public relations and advertising.

"One day at Kaiser, the Navy skit thing started all over again. The director of public relations called me into his office, handed me a Junior Achievement booklet and said, 'Your turn,' and I said, 'What do you mean?' and he said, 'Well, everyone else in the office has to do it and now it's your turn to do it. Form a group of young people and pick a project.'

"I took the booklet back to my desk and said, 'There's no way I can do this, I'm just not interested in it,' so I went back and said that I'd really prefer not to, and the boss said, 'Well, Larry, we've all had our turn and now it's your turn. That's the way it goes.'

"I went home to Rose that night and said, 'Man, I'm not going to run Junior Achievement, they can fire my ass.' I went in the next day and said I wasn't going to do it. I didn't get fired, but they had ways of letting me know I wasn't going to get anywhere at Kaiser Steel for a long time, if ever.

"After I'd worked at Kaiser for six months a letter came from the C.I.A. inviting me to go to work for them. So I quit Kaiser.

"The C.I.A. sent me to Africa in command of a group of Cuban mercenaries. There's not much I'm allowed to say about our mission, but when I look back, I'm really uneasy about what I was having them do. Even so, I get a great deal of satisfaction out of the way I was able to communicate with that group of men. Living in a small village in the Congo, we got down to basics. We said and did what we felt. We got the job done and a lot of those Cubans showed more skill and bravery almost every day than I had seen in the Navy.

"When the C.I.A. assignment was over, I gave in to a friend of mine with Pan Am who was constantly telling me, 'Goddamn it, Larry, with Pan Am you fly eighty hours a month, maybe ten, twelve days a month, and the rest of the time you're off. Twenty, thirty thousand dollars a year, all the free time you want.

"Well, Rose and I were living in Silver Spring, Maryland, and we both wanted to go back to San Francisco where we'd met. Pan Am offered me a job there, so I signed up.

"There were a lot of reasons why I wanted to be a Pan Am pilot. Part of it was the image thing, like I really dug being an airline pilot and what that said to people about me. I knew I was admired whenever I walked out to that airplane. Hell, when I was in the Navy I used to drive around in an MG with the top down and my hard hat and a copy of *Dr. Zhivago* on the back seat because I thought it was a great image. Wow!

"But in addition to the label thing, I wanted to be a good professional pilot the way a pro golfer or ball player is good. When I was flying for Pan Am, I was doing something I was good at, and enjoyed. I think if it hadn't been for the way it warped my family life, and the continual petty hassles, I might still be on that flight deck.

"It wasn't too long before I hated leaving home on those ten- and twelve-day trips. I hated the idea of leaving my family, and I hated the idea of not being there as my kids developed.

"When I was away, it was 3,000 miles away for almost two weeks at a time. I felt like I was 'uncle daddy,' when I'd come home—a guy who's just passing through to stay until his next trip. I'd waited until I was twenty-nine to get married and I wanted to enjoy my family."

For Rose Murphy, the mother of a three- and four-year-old son and daughter, the life of a pilot's wife forced her to live in "tomorrow," numbed her sex life, and brought her close to divorce every six months. "It was really difficult, always living in anticipation, only rarely being able to say or do what I felt 'now.' I'd have to say to myself, 'I'll have to remember to say that to Larry,' or 'I'll have to remember to tell Larry about this.' And we were always going to do something, 'when he got home,' and 'before this trip,' and 'after that trip.' I could only tell the kids that, 'daddy would be home in a few days.'

"Then, too, we're Catholic, and working the rhythm system with the Pan Am schedule was impossible. Larry and I figured out one time that we could only get together safely once every two months.

"Then every six months Larry had to take his flight checks and the strain made us both so edgy we were impossible to live with. Each time it came up his whole career with Pan Am was at stake. The pilots knew that any time the instructors wanted to fail them they could.

"It was like the strain of a doctor having to take his medical boards, or a lawyer having to take his bar exam again every six months. If you fail, that's it. I'm not saying it wasn't necessary, it probably was, but that didn't make it any easier to live with."

Larry Murphy passed his flight checks every six months during the four and a half years he was with Pan Am, and did his share of flying. Like any competent pilot who knows his equipment, he "wore" the airplane and it moved when and how he wanted it to. It wasn't any special strain from flying the airplane that drove him to his potter's wheel.

"Another thing that happened was back in 1964," he told me, "when Viet Nam was first becoming an issue in this country. Pan Am announced they would not force a pilot to fly to Viet Nam if he didn't want to, and at that time we had a lot of contract flights flying in and out of Saigon. When I first went with Pan Am I flew to Saigon, because I felt I wanted to do my part. But when my attitudes began to change I submitted a letter to the chief pilot and said I didn't want to fly to Viet Nam any more —I had even written to the Navy and resigned my commission as a protest against the war.

"The chief pilot called me in and gave me back the letter and said 'You can't put in a letter like that,' and I said 'what do you mean I can't? You have a provision to do that.' He told me 'We allowed people to send in letters until a certain date and we closed down the procedure after that,' and I said, 'You mean the guys who submitted letters then don't have to fly to Viet Nam, but I can't submit a letter now and I *have* to fly to Viet Nam?' and he said, 'That's right, you'll go where we tell you to go.'

"I told him I wasn't going to fly to Viet Nam and he said, 'If we tell you to go, you'll go.' But I was determined not to fly there and I talked about it to Rose and we agreed it would be better to quit. As it turns out, I never was told to fly to Viet Nam, so the issue never came to a head.

"I know I could have avoided a lot of those hassles if I had gone along with whatever system I was in; the Navy or Kaiser Steel or Pan Am or whatever. But I found that those things were destructive for me, that I was being pressured to be the kind of person I didn't want to be.

"I can't come down too hard on the guys in the system; maybe some day they'll go way past me in finding their own thing and doing it.

"When I was in the system I worked for guys who stole, or who did things in the office or the community because it would 'look good.' Thank God, I didn't do it.

"There were plenty of guys I saw in the CIA during my two years there, who were working twelve hours a day on GS-10 and -11 salaries because they really believed in what they were doing. I'm not saying I have a strong aversion to what they were doing. What bothered me was that there was nothing for *me* to believe in.

"I don't think you have security in the corporate system unless you buy it with your self-respect. When your boss and his boss can predict how you will react in any situation, then they can feel you fit into the corporation. The corporation can use you, you are a very fine, func-

tional tool for the organization, because you are just like
that big computer in the corner; you're predictable.

"That kind of pressure, to go along, to be predictable,
was destructive to me. But none of the pressures I felt,
or the incidents I've mentioned were the final thing that
made me leave Pan Am.

"What happened was a couple of days before I was
scheduled to leave on an eleven-day trip to Hong Kong.
I had this big, ugly rug that covered our whole living
room floor and the hall that was in the house when we
moved in. Rose and I wanted to get rid of it. I rolled it
up into a great big roll and a guy from down the street
and I dragged it out on the front porch and hefted it up
over the railing and it fell right down on our four-year-
old boy.

"We looked down and saw his feet sticking out from
underneath it. I didn't know if I had killed him or what.
As it was, all he had was a mild concussion. But he was
unconscious for some time and we were with him all
night and suddenly I realized, 'Shit, I'm going to Hong
Kong for eleven days. What kind of life is this? I'm never
home with my family. So I went in and quit.''

Rose Murphy says she was relieved when her husband
came home and said he'd resigned from Pan Am. "I
really felt good for Larry and myself. I remember Larry
telling me that while he was driving back home that day
he was saying to himself, 'What am I doing? What am I
doing? What will we do? What's going to happen?' And
at times I used to get that feeling, too, because I knew
we wouldn't have that Pan Am paycheck next month.

"Now new friends hear about it and say, 'Wow, what
you did!' but now that we're into being on our own, it
doesn't seem like it was such a big thing.''

Before the accident with his son, Larry hadn't set a

date for leaving Pan Am, although he knew he'd been working toward it in a way. "I was always artistic, always drawing; and I used to paint. Even in grammar school, and more in high school and college, I was the guy they brought things to to draw or paint. I was the school cartoonist and poster artist, and I took art courses.

"My art was considered 'a nice thing for Larry to do,' but it wasn't something I was encouraged to do.

"While I was with Pan Am I started taking courses in painting. When I got through the painting class I took drawing and then ceramics. The ceramics thing really grabbed me and I went into this feeling that, 'Gee, maybe some day I'll be able to develop this into a livelihood.' I knew it was a fantasy, but I still fantasized.

"Well, I got better and better and better and took pottery and started making things. People started buying my stuff at school and shopping-center art shows, and that did something."

Rose recalls that seven months before leaving Pan Am, Larry took his creations to a potters' association show, "And his things just sold and sold and sold, even though he was competing with a lot of professional, successful, and recognized potters. It was a morale booster for both of us, and such a satisfaction to set his things out and have people like them and be complimentary—and buy them."

Larry started traveling to San Francisco-area shopping-center art shows and other sales on weekends when he was home, and putting in full days' work at his basement potters' wheel, to build up his inventory, and to see how it felt to him to be working at pottery full time. "There were weeks," he says, "when I was more a potter than a pilot, and it felt good."

"Rose and I talked with other potters and craftsmen at

art shows and at potters' associations and calculated what I could produce and how much I'd be able to sell. We figured that, if I became a potter fulltime, I'd be able to make about $12,000 a year.

"About two months before leaving Pan Am, we started living on $1,000 a month, and putting the rest of my income, which came to about $20,000 a year, into savings. Once I was out, we ate more beans and didn't go out so much. But we didn't need two cars, and I wore blue jeans instead of uniforms, so our expenses were lower, too.

"When I quit, it wasn't as though we were completely unprepared. In a way, going in to resign might have been a *negative* thing to do; however, the overriding issue was that I *chose* pottery, I *chose* a way of life that I felt was best for *me.* So I look at it as an affirmative thing.

"There are a lot of people who quit well-paying jobs and it's probably a mistake if it's a negative thing, to *get away,* instead of to get *into* something they really want to do.

"When I could no longer take Pan Am, I was fortunate to have something that was really powerful and positive and demanding that I could say 'yes' to. I think the problem for most men who want to get out is not making a living—they can find a way to do that. It's that they've lost touch with their *feelings* about what's right for them. You can't live with the demands of the corporation without turning off your feelings to some extent, so you can't sense your gut reactions to things as well, can't tell what's right for you. I don't know how to solve that one.

"It's not easy to make a break. At first I tried to get furloughed by Pan Am. When you're furloughed you don't get paid, but keep your place on the seniority list and have a chance to go back. I think now that if I had been able to get a furlough, I would have failed as a potter. By quitting I was making a commitment and that commitment, taking the risk, makes a difference.

"There's a clipping I found someplace that I keep pinned to the wall by my potter's wheel. It says:

" 'Concerning all acts of initiative, there is one elementary truth, the ignorance of which kills countless ideas and splendid plans; that the moment one definitely commits oneself, then Providence moves, too. All sorts of things occur to help that otherwise never would have occurred. A whole stream of events issues from the decision, raising in one's favor all manner of unforseen incidents and meetings and material assistance. I have learned [says the author of this statement] deep respect for Goethe's couplet:

Whatever you can do, or dream you can, begin it.
Boldness has genius, power and magic in it.'

"I think that when it comes to taking responsibility for yourself, like leaving the system to manage your own life, a lot of couples have the tendency to put it off forever. We're trained to do that. We put things off until we've saved enough money, or until our kids are grown, or until we retire. Putting off living is a thing we're conditioned to do by the system. Rose and I planned for getting out, but we didn't agonize over it. There were some surprises."

Rose Murphy says she was anxious during their first few months. "But I was committed to what we were doing and knew I could always get a job, and that Larry could get a job. A lot of my middle-class expectations had changed and I didn't feel I'd be 'doing without' a lot of things we could have bought.

"The changes in Larry, and in our lives, were so

beautiful, though, that in the balance his leaving the company was a freeing thing, an opening up. It made for a kind of wholeness. Now there is this kind of total peace in our family life and work. Larry likes to work out in the garden and he can go from working in the garden to the kids and to his wheel.

"It wasn't anything we planned or tried to work out, so much time for this or so much time for that; it just started. Now we flow from one thing to the other as if there is a natural order to it—and I guess there is."

Larry and Rose admit there are problems when a husband and father is working at home most of the time. "It's something," he says, "that I've had to deal with very carefully so far as the kids are concerned. I've had to learn how to handle twenty-four hours a day togetherness with three kids who are very close in age and who constantly compete for attention: they compete for toys, for mommy's attention, and for daddy's attention all the time.

"Rose and I both had a lot of adjusting to do with my being around the house all day. I had to learn to discipline myself to the fact that just because I was home, it didn't mean I wasn't *working* and I had to tell myself, 'I'm at work,' and I had to go downstairs to work and not be distracted by a lot of other things."

Having Larry at home presented its own set of problems for Rose. "I didn't ask Larry to fix things for me when he was working, and I didn't want to feel that he was breathing down my neck all day, watching me. Having Larry home was a tremendous change from having him away for sometimes two weeks at a time. It was a bigger change for us than it would be for a couple where the husband was at least home every night.

"I had been autonomous and had been running the house on my own a lot of the time, being the man of the house along with being the mother and housewife. I had to run the house absolutely free of Larry's opinion about a lot of things. All of a sudden he was here *all* the time."

One of the things, say Larry and Rose, that made many of the difficult adjustments possible was that their sex life was so much better.

While he was with Pan Am, Larry says, "our sex life was really scheduled, like we'd make love the night I got home and the night before I left if the rhythm system said it was all right. Somehow, in that fragmented life, it seemed the natural thing to do, you get back together, you know, so you make love, or you're going to be away for ten days, so you make love if you can. It wasn't spontaneous.

"When you let a company inside your life like that, the way Pan Am's schedule invaded us, or the way a corporation's expectations of how an executive should live and what he should say, the company tends to live inside you and leave you less room to move around and get into yourself.

"We got into a more spontaneous sex relationship, for one thing, because we were both here and could let each other know how we felt and had a chance to do something about it. And when I didn't have the travel to face, and the captain to please, then I could be more myself and my feelings, including the sexual ones, just began to flow."

Rose feels their neighbors "probably think we fight more now and love each other less than we did for the first years we were here because it was very quiet in our house, and now they hear us shouting at each other and slamming doors and stuff. We love each other a lot more because we're more open with our feelings.

"We have fights now, but Larry and I think they're constructive fights. We've discovered that we used to interpret any kind of disagreement as withdrawal of affection, which was a threat because we felt we were insufficient. And when you've taken responsibility for yourself instead of just being a consumer, and you're living as a free person with a sense of dignity and living for yourself, you don't feel so insufficient any more.

"I think now that our children feel they have the same kind of freedom to express disagreement without either parent interpreting that as a withdrawal of affection."

Larry says that a lot of the things that he subscribed to for a long time on an intellectual level, are slowly becoming possible at a gut level. "Sometimes I still reach out and whack one of the children. Not that I think that's so bad, but I'd rather not seem to be teaching them that if you're bigger and stronger you can always get your way by flaunting your bigness and strength.

"Somebody once said that every time a parent exercises authority by force or violence he is admitting some failure, and it's true. If I can't get a kid to do something because he respects me, then I've got to admit his lack of respect, I guess. Usually I don't go through all that head trip, I just whack them. But at least I'm aware of what's going on.

"I can't explain how all this relates to being out of the corporate system, maybe it doesn't relate to it. The only thing Rose and I know is that we are seeing and feeling things we didn't see or feel before. I can't explain it. Sometimes the 'new Rose and Larry' crop up in some surprising ways that make us feel good.

"A few weeks ago a man we like called us up—he's a nice guy and he's single and likes to go out a lot. Rose and I don't go out much anymore; Rose made some excuses. After she got off the phone she said, 'I was really bullshitting that guy. I told him a big, damn lie.' She went back to the phone and called him up and said, 'You know, that was bullshit I just told you. We are tired and are looking forward to having an evening at home and we're not going out for that reason.' We were both high for a while on reaching the point where we could do that."

Larry spends his workday at his potter's wheel and kiln, coming upstairs for lunch with his wife, sometimes working for a few hours in the garden when it's sunny, and traveling occasionally to art shows to sell his pots. His income is a few thousand dollars above the $12,000 per year he and Rose felt they'd need to live. He gave his Pan Am pilot's cap to the boy next door and the only trace of his airline career is the pilot's black chart case he takes to art shows to carry change and a sandwich or two. A well-worn blue and white label on top says, "Pan Am Crew," but no one ever asks him about it.

5

Bill Neely: King of the Mountain

Jane Lew, West Virginia, about eighteen miles south of Clarksburg on State Highway 19 toward Weston, isn't one of those towns you can drive through without realizing you've ever been there. The road has too many twists and turns, and you've got to slow down long enough to spend a few minutes inside the city limits.

The land around Jane Lew is farming country. You can bring in a pretty good harvest of corn and maybe some asparagus, and raise cows for meat and milk. But the big cash crop around Jane Lew is coal, and bright green day-glo bumper stickers remind you to "Support Surface Mining," a posture that is under attack by environmentalists.

During the summer you can't miss the country music coming at you through open car windows and store front speakers from WHAW, Lewis County's 500-watt daytimer in nearby Weston.

For Bill Neely, coming back home to Jane Lew meant

being "king of the mountain" on the hill he had climbed as a kid, having the freedom to work his own farm and follow the stock car races and the Indianapolis 500, or to nourish his soul on the kind of jazz that first turned him on to music. It also meant that he could begin to support himself as a writer, on topics of his own choosing, at hours that suited his sense of family life, and without regard for corporate sensitivities about the clothes he wore, the car he drove, or the venality he was paid to conceal.

Before he decided to go home again, Bill Neely was a $20,000-a-year public relations executive for Humble Oil & Refining Company (now Exxon Corporation). He'd handled PR for the history-making Northwest Passage voyage of his employer's icebreaking tanker, S.S. *Manhattan,* had earned his company's gratitude and was in line for promotion when he walked into his boss's office and quit.

As we strolled around his farm, along cow paths, or through last fall's harvest of leaves, Bill Neely talked about days spent here years ago.

"From the time I was six or seven years old, I can remember coming up here with other kids, or just by myself and thinking what a beautiful place this was. This is the highest hill around here, or at least the highest hill with any road near it. You can see the place where I was born, and at night all the lights of Jane Lew.

"I had a great view from my forty-first floor office in the Humble Building in Houston, but it was like being inside a dragon looking out. I felt like if I got to the top I wouldn't like the kind of person I'd be when I got there."

Bill Neely grew up in Jane Lew. "In our town the kids

played the same games and went to the same places because there weren't that many places to go to or that many things to do. If the kids wanted to play baseball every kid in town played baseball because it took every kid in town to make a team.

"It wasn't until I went to college that I began to realize that I was a little different from the other kids. I think the fact that I went to college in the first place made me different because not many of the kids even finished high school, they just took on their fathers' farms."

By the time he was in his teens, Neely began to feel pressure from his family to compete as an athlete, mostly because his father was athletic. Not that he liked athletics, but "I thought it was something I should be doing."

"Our big rival in basketball then was Weston which was seven or eight miles away and about eight times bigger than Jane Lew. We rarely beat Weston in anything but we beat them in basketball one night. As a reward, my father took a good friend of mine and me to a spaghetti place in Clarksburg.

"But he never berated me when we lost, and I think that was one of the things, even at that early age, that allowed me to feel nothing was wrong with me if I wasn't turned on by sports.

"I also had a very good friend in high school with whom I used to spend a lot of time. He was someone I felt I could always be open with and to whom I could say anything I felt, no matter how crazy it was.

"Later on when I was president of my college fraternity, editor of the college newspaper, and still later when I was in public relations, I used to keep some of myself for *me*, and not try to be more like other people. I knew, working for big corporations, that I had to keep my feelings to myself. But I didn't feel bad about my feelings, nor did I think I should try to change."

As a boy, Bill Neely would often go to his father's hardware store, a sort of town meeting place, instead of getting into games with the other kids.

Most of the people there were older men, friends of his father's. Sometimes they came in to buy something, but most of the time they were just loafing. Bill enjoyed their company and listened to them swap stories about hunting or fishing or farming. "I think I picked up a desire to be with older people there, and going into the woods with some of those men I learned a love of the outdoors that's always stayed with me. I think for me the outdoors and nature is what is real, and that a lot of the things that people work hard for, status and so on, aren't real."

When it was time for college, two aunts he respected decided he should be a dentist, so he enrolled in a pre-med course at West Virginia University. The student body then was eight or nine thousand, and coming from a high school where an enrollment of three hundred seemed enormous, he was "really miserable." "I finished the semester there and transferred to West Virginia Wesleyan. Right away I gave up the thought of being a dentist and got started on what, in one way or another, has turned out to be my real work.

"I'd always admired my Uncle Dick, who was married to one of my twin aunts, and was a newspaperman on the Clarksburg *Telegraph*. So I got involved with the student newspaper at college and wound up as editor-in-chief. I got my first job after graduation on the same paper where my uncle worked."

Before long Bill Neely had a chance to go back to West Virginia Wesleyan as director of public relations. But when he got there he "could see all kinds of backbiting and political fighting going on.

"I knew I didn't want to spend a lot of time working to get to the top of that heap, and I didn't like being at the bottom of it either, so I got out as soon as I could.

"I finally got a public relations job with Goodyear in Akron. That job brought me to something I did love—cars. From the time I got out of college I was constantly buying and selling cars and more often than not I would make money on them.

"I suppose I've owned sixty or seventy cars. There were times when I'd own ten or fifteen cars in one year. I bought and sold so many cars one year I had to have a dealer's plates.

"Although I had a certain amount of fun at Goodyear, it wasn't long before I began to feel there were a lot of senseless things about corporate life that I was going to have to put up with.

"Often the rank and file PR men in our office were caught up in some of the petty politics going on between our bosses. Soon after I joined Goodyear one of the PR men was transferred back to Akron because he'd done less than a spectacular job in New York, and put over our division. He must have been feeling pretty defensive about it because he kept after my boss and all of us, nitpicking eveything we turned out.

"There was one guy in charge of publicity on a new kind of flooring we'd brought out, that had little flecks of gold in it. He'd said something in a release to the effect that 'all that glitters isn't gold,' because the product name had 'glitter' in it. Anyway, this ex-New York PR man sent the copy back with 'glitter' crossed out so the phrase read, 'All that glistens isn't gold.' It nearly drove us up the wall because every time a word like that was changed in a press release we'd have to start the rounds of departmental O.K.s again and then work overtime to meet deadlines.

"Our department, it seemed, was always on the edge of mutiny. It even got to the point where we had to sign out at lunch, listing where we were going, supposedly so they could get in touch with us. But it wasn't long before we were allowed to learn that some of the places we were eating were either too expensive—which meant the top executives ate there—or too low-brow to fit our company image.

"One of our problems was that we wanted to eat where the newspaper guys had lunch, and those places weren't exactly the most exclusive restaurants in town.

"I was aware that by going along with the lunch thing and by sending out press releases with writing I'd have been ashamed to put my by-line on as a newsman, I was selling out to a certain extent. But about the time it got really bad, I managed to get myself assigned to the field as Goodyear's specialist for racing publicity.

"I got to go to all the big races and all I had to do was make sure everybody had a drink or got a hotel room or got laid—plus turn out plenty of news releases and get them used.

"There were times, like when tires failed and killed drivers on the test track, that I had to keep Goodyear's name out of the newspapers, but I learned that's part of the PR game too—like later on, keeping Standard Oil or Humble's name from being mentioned when one of their tankers polluted the sea or one of their refineries pumped a lot of stuff into the river.

"Soon after I started handling Goodyear's race publicity the company started wanting a story on every race, along with a story and a picture of a tire and I finally had to tell them, 'Look there's only so much you can say about a tire and we sometimes have two races a day out here. If I try to keep that kind of thing going our releases will end up in the wastebasket without even being opened.' But they never really understood and always wanted more.

"Hectic as it was, I don't think I could ever have hoped to marry and settle down if it hadn't been for that job with Goodyear. I got rid of a lot of my restlessness during that period. The job let me follow the races, which I loved, and although I had to work damned hard, I had a girl at every track and a generous expense account.

"If there is such a thing as the *Playboy* life, I lived it. There were plenty of parties, usually a couple after every big race, and there was the feeling of being on the 'inside' of what I felt was one of the glamorous and exciting games going. My friends and I had pit passes and we drank beer with the drivers. Celebrities, movie stars, politicians, and so on, came to us when they wanted to meet a driver or get an autograph for their kids.

"And the women who dig racing really are like the ones you see in *Road and Track;* with sexy figures and clothes and ideas to match. There were some guys I knew who won races on sheer guts just because of what one of those women had promised if they came in first.

"But there got to be a time, living that kind of life, when I felt I couldn't keep it up any longer and wanted to settle down in a place I really liked with someone I really cared for. It was like I'd had all the cake and ice cream I could eat and still needed a good steak. Before meeting Martina I'd always stayed away from the idea of marriage. Soon after I got to know her, however, I realized *she* was what I needed and what had been a great and exciting life on the road became a drag.

"Martina and I got married in 1965, and although my life started to open up, my job came crumbling down around my feet because the company wouldn't take me off the road.

"I'd never had any great goals for myself as a high-level executive. When I was with Goodyear I realized that I'd rather have time off than a raise. I wanted to start at $10,000 a year for five days work, and after five years be getting $10,000 a year for three days work.

"But they made it clear to me that there wasn't room at Goodyear for anyone who felt that way. The corporate pipelines need people who can be promoted and if you don't consider working longer hours, giving up more of your private life, and moving up to more things you can't afford as 'getting ahead,' a corporation doesn't have space for you on the treadmill. You have to get off so someone else can have your place.

"I suddenly awoke to find that I was married, with two children, and working for a corporation that thought of me as something to be moved from race to race to race —forever. My last year with Goodyear I was away from home two hundred and fifty nine days and could see my marriage going right down the drain. The only thing I could do was look for another job.

"An employment agency I got in touch with set up an interview with Humble Oil & Refining Company in Houston, Texas. That company was to show me just how mixed up a corporation can be.

"While I was with Goodyear I'd gotten the idea I'd like to be a field PR man. I'd be free of day-to-day supervision, and there'd be less travel so I'd at least know what town I was in when I woke up in the morning.

"During interviews at Humble they told me I'd have a couple of years in the home office to learn the business and then be assigned as a field PR man. Just what I wanted. The pay was more than I'd been making at Goodyear so there wasn't any reason not to take the offer.

"I bounced around from desk to desk the first three weeks in Houston and one day the boss called me in and said, 'You're our new PR man in Memphis.' But no one, as yet, had told me anything about the petroleum industry or about Humble. So I spent my time in the company library reading children's books on the subject, about the only level of explanation I could understand at that point.

"More than a little disappointed, I went off to manage public relations for a region comprising Tennessee, Kentucky, Mississippi, Louisiana, Arkansas, Alabama, and the panhandle of Florida.

"They'd never had a PR man there before, and the regional manager thought the whole idea was absurd to begin with.

"But I got out and contacted the media, and they began using our news releases—something most newspapers in the area had never done before. Word got back to Houston and the PR manager there thought it was great. I was getting around.

"All I had was a children's-book knowledge about the oil business and practically no knowledge at all about Humble, but I did know enough to get out and call on newspapers and radio and TV stations so they'd know I was there. This was travel all over again, but I figured it would be worth it if I could do a decent job. And, of course, I wouldn't have to keep it up forever.

"But about the time I really got things rolling, one of my local bosses phoned my boss in Houston to complain that I was driving a Chrysler Imperial while he only had a Buick; that I was out working with the press instead of attending sales meetings. And my boss in Houston was unhappy because this man was complaining.

"I figured, 'What the hell, let them fight it out,' and went on doing my job. I went down to Birmingham and told the district manager I was there and would be contacting the media. He said they hadn't written anything about us for five years and that it wouldn't do any good, but I went anyway.

"When I walked into a newspaper office the guy there said, 'Well, it's about time,' and I said, 'What do you mean?' and he said that when Humble came into the area, 'I wanted to know what you were doing and how many people you'd be hiring, so I wrote a letter and they replied that they would refer me to the public relations department and that I would hear from you shortly. It's taken you four years to get here.'

"So I said, 'Why don't we have a drink and talk about this' and he said he'd be glad to have a drink with me, but that he didn't think it would change the way he felt about the company. Four martinis later he agreed that things like that could happen and we were good friends; he started using our news releases pretty regularly after that.

"I ran into this sort of thing in all our important marketing areas in the region. Houston thought I was doing great, but the regional bosses couldn't see any relationship between good media relations and sales, although they were the ones who came screaming to public relations to keep embarrassing things like pollution and labor trouble and accidents out of the press when they leaked out. You can't do that unless you have good *personal* relations with the media, because if and when they do keep a company name off the front page they're doing it for you, rather than for the corporation.

"But in spite of my getting the job done, that man was still on my back about the car thing and always after me to spend more time at sales meetings—often to help set up chairs and signs and stuff like that—so I went back to Houston one day and said, 'Look you got me into this, you get me out.' So my boss moved me back to Houston.

"When I got back there, it was like all of a sudden I'd died and gone to PR heaven. Humble was getting ready to send the icebreaking tanker S.S. *Manhattan* through the Northwest Passage; the first time anything like that had been done, *if* it could be done. It was the most spectacular thing any corporation ever attempted.

"We used to get phone calls from *Life* and the *National Geographic* and the TV networks asking if they could please send someone on the trip and could we please send them some pictures, and would it be possible to set up some interviews. The gates opened up and everyone wanted to run our story.

"But again the company had to complicate things. The day, the very *day*, the S.S. *Manhattan* sailed for the Northwest Passage, Humble sent the head of the media relations section on vacation and he didn't come back until after the ship arrived in Alaska.

"So with our boss away on vacation and our section shorthanded, we worked day and night and often weekends getting our story in the morning and evening editions of nearly every major paper in the U.S. and had the TV networks running our news clips so often you'd think the S.S. *Manhattan*'s trip was a daily TV series, which, in a way, it was.

"A new man with the company who'd been around the news business for quite a while set up the first corporate audio news service ever, and had voice reports from the ship on coast-to-coast radio stations almost every day. He also placed the first Sunday magazine news release, about eight-hundred words and twenty pictures, in nearly forty papers, again, the first time ever for any corporation. It's a good thing he didn't know enough to clear his ideas with top management or they'd probably never have got off the ground.

"Even this much was too good to last. Right in the middle of all this beautiful publicity the most astounding thing took place that's ever happened to me in sixteen or seventeen years in public relations: word came down that Humble's board had decided we were getting too much publicity, that maybe it didn't look good in the eyes of the other oil companies who also had leases in Alaska. So we were told to 'cool it' on the publicity. It was like telling someone on the race track, 'Look, you're ahead and you're making the other guys look bad,' I couldn't believe it.

"The ship made it back to New York and newsmen there said it was the biggest press conference they'd been to since the opening of the United Nations.

"But when the S.S. *Manhattan* sailed into New York harbor all my hopes of doing anything creative for the company sailed out past her. My last assignment on the day of the news conference was when one of the PR section heads told me to 'Go stand over there and be sensitive to the escalator.' So I stood at the top of the escalator on Pier 83 in New York looking down at the company officials and their wives who came for a quick visit to a ship that had returned from one of the few parts of the world where their corporate ambition had yet to take its toll.

"The S.S. *Manhattan* came back in November of 1969 and in January, 1970, Congress reduced the 27 1/2 percent oil and gas depletion allowance to 22 percent. Humble immediately reorganized its PR department and Government Relations department into a combined Public Affairs department.

"The previous PR manager was retired and the company appointed a new man to head the combined departments. Suddenly nobody in a top position affecting me had any obvious experience in media relations or PR. It got so the PR professionals working there found it impossible to get anything done because we were always having to teach 'PR 101' to our bosses.

"I remember one thing that made me decide to get out as soon as I could. Late one afternoon we were sitting around the office trying to get out a news release on a price increase.

"The thing had been going around for approvals for a couple of days and we were into the thirty-fifth draft with vice presidents in the office when one of them asked the PR manager if we could get the release out that night. He turned to me and I said, 'Yes, we'll put it on the PR Newswire,' so my boss said, 'Well, fine, we'll put it on the PR Newswire tonight.'

"The PR Newswire is a New York outfit that has teletype machines just like AP and UPI in nearly every major newspaper and radio and television station in the coun-

try. The machines are put there for free, and PR Newswire uses them to feed their clients' news releases,
speeches, and press conference announcements all over
the country.

"A lot of PR Newswire's material is good solid news;
like maybe a car company's announcement on a reduced
pollution engine or a politician's statement on a hot issue
or some university's new scientific discovery. Newspapers like PR Newswire too, because the copy is edited
into newspaper style, correctly spelled and punctuated.
If I had something really important to the company, the
response of Humble's president to Congressional hearings some afternoon, for example, I could phone his
statement to PR Newswire and it would be at hundreds
of newspapers within thirty minutes, in time for use the
same day as the hearings instead of two or three days
later as it would be if we'd mailed it out.

"Well, anyway, I said we'd put the price increase story
on the PR Newswire that night, and *everybody* in public
relations knows what the PR Newswire is. Yet after the
meeting is over and we're out in the hall, one of my new
bosses takes me aside and asks, 'Say, what's the PR Newswire?' I think that was the final thing that made me make
up my mind to leave.

"I'd somehow never quite lost touch with what was
real to me, and what I liked for me, no matter what
anyone else thought. At Humble I saw what happened to
men who didn't like themselves for what they had to do,
and I knew I had to start feeling good about the work I
did each day and how I lived each week when it was over.

"I saw our board members, old men mostly, drive to
and from work in closed company Cadillacs, isolated
from the traffic and the people and the wind and the sun,

and ride up to their mausoleums on the forty-second floor where conversations were conducted almost in whispers. They were out of touch with the real world and didn't associate with anyone who lived in it.

"Few people in our office ever seemed to do a spontaneous thing in their lives, at least so far as I could see. They were afraid of their jobs and afraid of themselves, thinking about saying, in a meeting, whatever would make points, rather than what might solve the problem we were supposed to be there to resolve.

"This is the place I found myself in and it was getting so bad I had to turn myself off when I went to work every day. It was getting harder and harder to turn myself on again each time I got back home, so I got out.

"I had to ask myself what I really loved most. Myself, my wife and family, the outdoors, that hill in Jane Lew. And I liked jazz and country music and cars, just about any car you could name.

"I realized one way I could have all that, and do the work I enjoy, which was to write—to write about auto races and music, some of the men who *are* racing and who make the music. So I thought I'd write, and if I failed, I'd farm. I knew I'd do anything before I'd stay where I was. So I quit.

"There wasn't anything spectacular about it. I finally resigned one Friday because I couldn't think of anything that would brighten my weekend more than quitting Humble.

"I went into the PR director's office and said, 'Look I've been thinking a long time and I've been working pretty hard and I've decided to retire,' and he said, 'What do you mean?' and I said, 'Well, I'm going back to West Virginia and get a farm and do some farming and write a bit at my own pace and enjoy the rest of my life.'

"Well, I was thirty-nine at the time, and hadn't even been a manager yet and I don't think anyone at work had any idea of what I was talking about when I said I was quitting to do exactly what I wanted to do. They all seemed to think doing what you want was for when you're old, and maybe not even then. So anyway we shook hands and later on there was a little party but so far as my resignation itself, that was it.

"Martina and I went out and got a bottle of champagne and drank it and the next day we put an ad in the paper to start selling things, not that we had all that much to sell, but we knew we'd need every bit of money we could lay our hands on.

"We'd made and saved a few dollars when we sold our house in Memphis and we added to that by selling Martina's nearly new Mustang and my mint condition Mercedes 190-SL, some photographic equipment and some miscellaneous stuff. So there we were, every day getting rid of things we'd worked hard for and sacrificed to get, happy as kids on Christmas morning each time we sold one of those things, because each sale was a step to freedom.

"Altogether, we started out with less than six months living expenses in our pocket when we left Houston for Jane Lew. I had a wife, two pre-teen-age daughters and a son less than six months old; didn't have a job and didn't know if I'd make it as a writer, but we were singing when we left the city limits. I didn't think about it as we headed the Chrysler Imperial east, but it was the only time since I'd learned to drive that I was down to one car."

Soon after he'd returned to Jane Lew and found a small rented house to live in, Bill Neely began working at becoming an author. "An editor I knew at *Sports Illustrated* suggested I propose a book on Craig Breedlove, the high-performance auto designer and driver, to a Chicago publisher he'd written for. Breedlove, in case you don't know, had set the world land speed record in his car, *The Spirit of America,* and was a colorful character in his own right, as well as a hell of a designer, mechanic, self-taught engineer and driver. I didn't know the first thing about how you propose a book to a publisher, but he explained what a book outline is and I began to put one together. The outline, I learned, should contain what I was going to include in each chapter, plus something about how I planned to handle certain episodes in Craig's life.

"The publisher liked the outline and signed a contract for me to write the book. So, at least in a legal sense, I had become an author. The publisher's advance against royalties wasn't much more than two months' salary at Humble, but to me it said I'd be able to make it outside the rat race.

"The Breedlove book was a modest success, and I did a second book on stock-car racer Richard Petty. We lucked out on the Petty book because just as we were ready to bring the book out, Petty became the first stock car driver to earn a million dollars in winnings. The next book, on jazz, my second or maybe sixth love (depending on how you add cars, a wife and three kids) was a biography, so to speak, of Pete Fountain, the jazz clarinetist who owns a club in New Orleans.

"I'm working on a couple of other books now, plus one with my friend from *Sports Illustrated.* I've done a couple of pieces for *Playboy,* one on Breedlove and one on fear, plus some articles for the auto and racing magazines.

"The books I do aren't 'big' books, they'll never be best sellers and most people will probably never hear about them, but I'm writing about what I like, making a living, and I don't have anyone, other than my family and myself, making decisions about my life.

"After I finished the Petty book and signed the contract for *A Closer Walk,* the Pete Fountain book, Martina and I felt it was probably O.K. to get a place of our own. A fifty-four-acre piece of land that included my hill plus a hundred-year-old, four-bedroom house, had been for sale since we'd come back to Jane Lew, but I was afraid to even think about that place for fear someone would pick up my vibes and buy it before we could.

"It wasn't especially cheap as property goes around here, $11,000, but we wanted *that* piece of land. We put down our money and moved in less than two years after leaving Humble. Since then we've added a hundred-and-thirteen-acre piece of adjoining property and my friend from *Sports Illustrated* bought a twenty-seven-acre place with a small house for barely $5,000.

"The house is taking work to get into first-class shape, but it's nothing Martina and the kids and I can't do ourselves. It's more labor than money that's needed.

"We've enough room now to invite a lot of the people I interview to visit with us here, so although I'm writing more, I'm traveling less. Most of the people who've visited seem to enjoy working with me around the place, so we become more of an extended family than just people doing part of a book with each other."

Bill Neely reminded me that when we'd started talking I'd asked if he'd been a loner. "I've never quite been a loner," he said. "I guess you could call me more of a 'oner.' Though I've never liked crowds and hated being a number, I've always wanted one other person around all the time. If I was going to drive across town I'd talk someone into going with me just to have someone to talk to. I've always hated being completely alone.

"The whole corporate life defeated my desire to pick the people I spend my time with. For me it's better to work with people I like than with people a company has just stuck in an office with me.

"Before I got out, I'd never thought much about my thing of not being alone, but now I feel that perhaps I didn't want to face myself or confront what I was doing with my life—that always having someone along made it easier to avoid getting in touch with 'me.' Now I like the person I can be, so I'm not afraid of a discovery I might make about myself when I'm alone. I can be comfortable walking alone on my hill, doing work around the place, or driving. I see things now I never saw before and touch things that never touched me when I was in the rat race.

"It sounds almost petty, talking about the things that went on at Humble, being concerned about them; and yet that's part of the trap we get into. So many guys in corporations like Humble have come to accept that kind of stuff as part of their lives, thinking that's the way it has to be.

"The fact is, it's *not* the way it has to be. What those guys don't know is that every time they give in a little bit to the corporate way of being, they're killing a little bit of themselves. If they wonder why the joy and the warmth and the feeling have gone slowly out of their lives, *that's why.*

"Even though the boss wasn't following me around every day, in some respects he might as well have been. I had to get up when the company wanted me to, do my job the way they wanted me to, associate with the people they wanted me to, dress the way they wanted me to, and speak the thoughts they wanted me to—at least in public.

"When I quit Humble, with one step, *in one hour,* I took back control of my life. Today my calendar and my hours are my own. I work when I do my best work and spend my time with people I really like. Some people I know say that's selfish, but it's what is best for *me* and *my* family.

"I still earn my living working almost every day, probably more hours in a year than I put in before. On days when I'm writing at home I get up at five or six and type until Martina and the kids are up. After the kids are in school Martina and I have some time just for us, something we never had before until the kids were in bed each night—not exactly a person's best hours.

"Sometimes Martina and I will go shopping or blitz the house or do the laundry or go back to bed and make love. Usually about eleven I'll go back to my desk and write for another four hours till the girls get home from school. When they're home from school I have time to be with them when that's what they want, or maybe work on the house or do something around the place like fixing the tractor or mending some fence.

"When I need to, I'll write in the evening, otherwise just be with the kids and Martina for whatever we feel like doing. When I'm working Martina doesn't bother me with household stuff, but she's aware I'm close and I feel her, there, too.

"Martina and I are usually together when I'm out on the road on interviews for a book or magazine articles I'm writing. We don't feel too bad about being away from home sometimes like that because we can both be with the kids so much when I am at home. We feel that as far as the family is concerned, things couldn't be better."

Martina Neely appreciates what she calls a "full-time

husband," and says she's relieved, too, to have her children out of urban schools and away from some of the problems of big city life.

"Bill may be making less than we would have earned if he'd stayed at Humble," she says, "but in a corporation like that, every time you earn more, there's always someone to tell you how to spend it. You're expected to get a bigger house, or a bigger car, or send your kids to a certain school or join certain clubs, so there's no real gain.

"To get our kids out of Houston we'd have had to spend more for a place to live and Bill would have had to spend a lot of time and money commuting. Our whole farm cost less than a surburban house in Houston and Bill doesn't have to commute. So while we're living on less, we're enjoying it more."

I asked Bill Neely if he didn't think his case was a little unusual, made easier, perhaps, by the fact that he seemed to be creative; he could write and a lot of insurance salesmen, accountants, and other people couldn't do that. He said, "You're right about part of it, I did get out, but don't forget that there are thousands of guys in public relations and thousands more in advertising and working for newspapers and radio and TV stations who can probably write a hell of a lot better than I can. There are probably a lot of accountants and insurance salesmen who can also write better than I can.

"When it comes to creativity, I think we all have it, or at least, we had it before it was squeezed out of us by the system. Look, I didn't have my first book sold when I quit my job. We just figured if we sold almost everything we had, we could get by until something worked out. It happened to be the book, but that isn't the point.

"I know it sounds crazy, but I think that if you just get out, the creativity comes. Maybe not *writing* creativity, but some kind of creativity related to something you already know about, so you can make your way and enjoy it.

"I doubt I was free enough with my feelings while at Humble to have been able to write a book. I was having to hold my feelings in so much around the office; having to avoid saying what I felt, having to avoid acting as I felt and even having to avoid making friends with certain people at work I would have liked to know. That creativity was too deeply buried for me to feel.

"It was only after I broke out of Humble that I was free enough with my feelings to do the creative things I'd been capable of."

"Sometimes you've got to take a risk and try what looks impossible. They say you can't go back home again, but I *am* back home again, back on this hill and back home with myself."

6

Ralph Graham: Climbing Down the Ladder of Success

I telephoned Ralph Graham after being given his name by friends in Miami. Ralph, they told me, was a rapidly rising, thirty-six-year-old engineer-manager at North American Aviation when he'd taken leave of absence to earn his master's degree in oceanography. He'd since decided never to return to industry and in the fall of 1972, was still working on his Ph.D. in psychology.

We talked in the back of the small house he rents on the inland waterway in Del Ray Beach, Florida, with only the sound of an occasional yacht churning by to interrupt us. Ralph began to express some of his feelings about life in the corporate world.

"The fantasy is that you can live with the system and still have other things, but you can't do it and still have yourself because the industry image is that any company is a happy family. If you try and exclude yourself from that family, you will find yourself being pushed out."

For a time during his five years with North American,

Ralph Graham was willing to pay almost any price for corporate advancement. He earned an engineering degree when he'd rather have majored in the humanities, became a top-flight project manager, learned to play company politics, worked on missiles that could wipe out an entire city, and became a corporate hatchet man, ending the careers of men who were more capable, but less "politically astute" than he was.

In time, he said, the moral issues caught up with him. His advancement within the company left him less and less time for himself and the life he'd hoped to attain through the increasing freedom he'd thought an executive position would give him.

As a young engineer fresh out of college, Ralph Graham's entry into the system was an easy one and held more rewards than he expected to earn so early in the game. He managed to avoid the usual aerospace industry basic training at the drafting board and started in the field, testing rocket engines for the Atlas missile.

From testing rocket engines, Ralph Graham moved through five promotions at North America in as many years, working on Atlas engine installations in North American's Rocketdyne Division at San Diego, supervising field representatives and technicians on the Thor missile program at Vandenberg AFB, California, traveling as trouble shooter and "hatchet man," serving as assistant field manager for North American at Forbes AFB, Topeka, Kansas; and as an executive assistant before taking a one-year leave of absence to study oceanography at San Jose State College.

"All along," Ralph Graham says, "I'd wanted power and I'd wanted money, but with my final assignment as executive assistant for base activation, setting up our facilities at military bases all over the country, I realized that each promotion meant less and less freedom.

"What opened my eyes was when I took the headquarters job and one of the top executives at North American told me that I needed to buy a house in a specific price range in San Fernando Valley, that I needed to drive a different kind of car, wear the right kind of clothes and go to the right kind of parties.

"When I heard that I said to myself 'No.' From the time I was a kid I'd had this drive to acquire power and money and freedom. Now I was being offered a promotion with more money and power than ever and I didn't want it. Those things, power and money, were supposed to be the system's rewards for performance, but I'd been under pressure to perform for so long, even from my parents when I was five years old, that all I wanted to do now was break free. That offer of a promotion started turning wheels in my head, but it took a couple of other things to shift the wheels into high gear.

"I think a lot of where I was with myself at North American began a long time before that. In the first place, my father was an engineer and I'd felt some compunction to meet his expectations so far as my work was concerned. Secondly, he traveled a lot and I was left home with a mother who really wanted me to excel in some way. She decided I was going to be a lawyer or a concert pianist or a doctor and when I was about five I was slapped in front of a piano.

"I hadn't shown any musical talent that I know of, but I had five years of piano lessons and was geared by my mother to practice, practice, practice. I also learned to play the flute, the piccolo, English horn, the clarinet, and the bassoon.

"All the time I was learning to play musical instruments, I saw it as a work thing, and achieved a certain amount of recognition for it. But music wasn't my thing, and the recognition came from *outside* and not inside. Recognition never came from my parents because no matter how well I did, it was not good enough. If I had a concert and got three encores, it was, 'Why didn't you get four?'

"My father was a hunter and outdoorsman, and being a male child, I wanted to go hunting. But his idea of taking me hunting or fishing was that it was my job to take care of the camp, wash the dishes, and pack the tent and sleeping roll. After I did all the chores then I could fish.

"On deer-hunting trips we'd go off to the wilderness in the middle of winter, get out at four or five in the morning and find ourselves sitting in a blind waiting for a deer to come walking along and then we were supposed to blow its head off.

"Instead of thinking, 'Oh, boy, here I am, I'm a male and I'm something,' I was saying to myself, 'What the hell am I doing out here freezing my ass off at five o'clock in the morning getting ready to shoot a poor, defenseless animal who hasn't anything to say about it?'

"I guess you could say it was the first time I had some feelings of 'Their system is not my system.'

"From the time I was eight or nine, I went to summer camp where we swam and canoed and had a good time. But even there I got a lot of pressure from my father to learn how to paddle a canoe. His, and I guess *my* ultimate goal then, was for me to be able to guide a canoe down one of the northern trout streams using a paddle in one hand and be able to fly fish with a rod in the other hand,

and also keep the canoe oriented so that whoever was in the bow could fish whenever he wanted to.

"I was finally able to do this, hands down, no problem. It was an achievement, but that's all it was. There was no *fun* in it, and what might have been play became *work* because of the pressure from my parents.

"My mother died when I was eleven and about the same time my father lost his job. He went into business as manufacturer's representative for a bunch of sporting goods companies, so I ended up living alone from the time my mother died until I was a junior in high school when I was sent to a private school.

"During that time, I mostly lived alone in the family house, cooking my own meals, maintaining the house, and so on. There was a lady who taught me how to bake bread and make pies. And before she died, my mother taught me how to iron, clean the house, and take care of my own clothes.

"I began to realize then that my mother and father had done a lot of things to make me self-sufficient, but there were lots of things missing from my life that I needed even more—like love and affection.

"Right after my mother died, I got a job at night in a place that was a combination restaurant and dairy. I made ice cream, bottled milk, washed bottles, and also worked the soda fountain. Some mornings I also got up at three or four o'clock and delivered milk.

"My mother and father were church-goers and up until the time we moved to Charlotte, Ohio, when I was four, they had always been Methodists. But once after leaving the only Methodist church in Charlotte, I heard my father saying to my mother, "Well, next Sunday I guess we ought to go to some other church,' and my mother saying it seemed like a good idea, *because they hadn't liked a new minister.*

"All this time, I was sitting in the back seat saying to myself, 'How come if this church thing is such a big deal and we're supposed to be Methodists, we suddenly decide we're going to some different church because we don't like the minister?'

"When we started going to a different church I began to feel I might need a confidante, and that the minister of this new church might fill the bill. From the ninth grade on I used to go and talk to him, and he was willing to stay up until three or four in the morning whenever I had something on my mind.

"Through this minister, I began to look at a lot of the traditional values like: why do people get married? and why do people get stuck in what seemed to me to be ruts like getting up and going to work and coming home?

"Well, one day during my junior year in high school, a friend of mine came over and we decided to look at some of the guns in my father's collection. My friend accidentally shot himself in the hand, and his parents wrote a letter to the juvenile court saying it was bad that I was being allowed to live by myself, that I was going to hell and that something ought to be done. So, my father had to send me off to private school.

"In spite of my wanting to go to a military academy, I was sent to the Cranbrook School in a suburb of Detroit, one of the most exclusive schools in the country.

"I couldn't work at the school, however, so I had no money, and everybody around me had more money than I'd ever seen in my life.

"The parking lot of this school looked like a new car showroom. Most of the kids who went there had fathers who worked in the automotive industry, so they had new Fords and new Chevys and I didn't have even a bicycle or any way of getting one.

"I didn't know how to dress and the clothes I had were nothing. I had this cheap sport coat that looked like camel's hair but wasn't, and one day, this kid came up and said, 'Hey that's some jacket, where did you get it?' and before I could say anything he was reaching inside my coat looking for a label.

"Well, it had come from Sears and Roebuck and at that time, I guess, Sears and Roebuck didn't put labels on their coats. This turned out to be a real disaster for me because in that school a coat without a label just wasn't a coat.

"So talk about resenting the system; within *two weeks* I had myself screwed down until I didn't show anything: no feelings, no emotions, no nothing, and I made up my mind then and there that I was going to have money and tell the world to fuck off.

"I finally made friends with two other kids who were at Cranbrook on scholarships and didn't have any money either. We soon learned how to sneak off weekends, roamed around Detroit, and made friends with outside kids and got into gang wars.

"It dawned on me about that time I had two choices as far as my life was concerned. One was to become a criminal, and the other was to climb the ladder in an accepted manner, because the two things I wanted then were *status* and *money,* and I really didn't care how I got them.

"I think even then I had some intuitive sense that there wasn't a hell of a lot of difference between being a criminal outside the law and being a businessman inside it. It was obvious that as a criminal the law was going to be after you, but I never saw this in terms of good and bad.

"I ended up in so much trouble at Cranbrook that I had to leave at the end of the year and finally got to go to a military school, Saint John's Military Academy at Delafield, Wisconsin.

"When I got to Saint John's, I was *home free*. First of all, they had a system of rewards for getting good grades, so I got rewarded for what I could do well.

"It also turned out that the captain and the first sergeant of the company I was in had trouble with science and math and I was good in science and math. So I helped them and got all kinds of privileges in the company.

"While I was there, I got in touch with another thing I wanted besides money and status; that was *power*. It seemed to me that one way to be *free* was to be in *control*. I was learning that you didn't necessarily have to have *authority* to have power; sometimes it was enough if you knew how to *manipulate*.

"Later on, I came to realize that's not the way to be free. If you're in control, like the king and slave story, there may be all these people bowing and scraping, but it's pretty lonely.

"The next fall, almost at the last minute, I enrolled at Michigan State and was put in a dormitory with a bunch of Korean War veterans who were going to be engineers. My father was also an engineer and I felt he wanted me to do something like that. I also knew there was such a shortage of engineers that if you had an engineering degree you could write your own ticket. I wanted money and was good in math and science so it all seemed to mesh.

"Michigan State had this basic core program so that all freshmen and sophomores had four basic courses, social science, English, natural science and humanities. I got C's in math and science and A's in my social science and humanities courses.

"I was turned on by my humanities courses where classes tended to become discussion groups, whereas in my math and science courses it was 'memorize this equation' and 'memorize that formula.' So I ended up that first year thinking maybe I ought to change my major.

"About this time my father died, so maybe I felt under a little less pressure to meet any expectations he may have had.

"For a while, I sort of fumbled around. I majored in journalism one semester and I took a course in logic and a course in philosophy. I liked all those courses but kept having this feeling that humanities professors were starving to death and engineers were making money hand over fist. I wanted money so I said to myself, 'O.K. I'm committed to becoming an engineer.'

"I went through engineering school *hating* every goddamned minute of it, bound and determined I was going to get through. I finally graduated with a 2.19 average. That's barely over a C. Even with a C average, just the fact that my degree said 'engineer' on it meant that I had thirty-five interviews and got thirty-five job offers.

"When I graduated I didn't know what I *wanted* to do, but when I got to talking with some of those companies I knew what I *didn't* want to do.

"Some companies said they'd put me on the drafting board for six months and then I could start being a real engineer, and I said, 'But I don't want to be an *engineer*. I want to work with *people*.' They said 'What did you

major in engineering for?' and I would say, 'I really don't
know.'

"In all those thirty-five companies I talked to I only
found two people who really 'came on' for me. One of
them worked for International Telephone and Telegraph and he said, 'You're going to have a tough time all
your life. The reason is you're multitalented and have a
lot of capabilities and I really don't know that you're ever
going to be happy working for a company.'

"This blew my mind because until that time I had
never really considered *not* working for a company—
because the companies had the power.

"The other guy I ran into during interviews who was
kind of where I was with respect to the corporate world,
worked for Standard Oil of Indiana, and he said, 'I don't
think I have a job for you and I don't think you're ever
going to find a job that you will be happy with. I want you
to be aware that when you go to work for a corporation
you're going to have to give up a little of yourself. I'm
sorry that you're going to have to do it, but if you go to
work for a corporation that's what's going to happen.'

"Well, I took a job with North American Aviation
primarily because that guy interviewing me said, 'O.K.
there'll be no time on the drawing board,' and he put me
in the field service end of the business. The first six
months I was in one of their training programs testing
rocket engines and I thought I would go out of my mind
because part of the training was tearing down rocket
engines. I worked as a mechanic, which I couldn't care
less about.

"The other part of my training was learning to test
rocket engines where you were in the blockhouse and
put on a microphone and pushed all the buttons which

meant that the thing went 'zap' and ran like it was supposed to, or it blew up and you had to tear it down to maybe see what went wrong. Then you did the same thing again the next day. To me this was all pretty boring.

"I was seriously considering moving on when they took me out of the training program and sent me to the Rocketdyne Division in San Diego where North American was installing engines in the Atlas missile. This was a pretty good situation. First, my personality was neat for this sort of thing and I was able to work well with these people, some of whom were highly educated engineers and some of whom were technicians and mechanics short of formal schooling, but they knew how things *worked.*

"I learned to play politics well enough so that I soon started getting promoted. I'd gone to San Diego in September of 1957 and was moved up to Vandenberg Air Force base in June of 1958. I worked on the THOR program at Vandenberg and had ten people working for me, two field reps and eight technicians. All I had to worry about was that they were doing what they were supposed to do. I had good people who were willing to cover for me—and I was willing to cover for them—so I could give myself some free time. So far the system wasn't so bad, in fact, considering where I'd been, it was beautiful.

"Anyway things went along pretty good in this situation and I got called back to the home office for a promotion to staff assistant to the supervisor of base activation. I was supposed to deal with the movement of personnel; who was supposed to go where, what kind of people they were and this sort of thing; not so much with the technical end of the business.

"I started going to a lot of military bases checking on how people were performing, and when there was a problem they'd send me to find out who was at fault and ax them. I was very effective at this. I pretty well knew the ball game by then and had a lot of insight as to who needed to be removed to make things right for the company.

"But what was happening to me was this: For the first time I began to consider people as *individuals* rather than as parts of a 'subsystem.'

"I axed people who had come with North American about the same time I had, who were not much older, and who were sometimes smarter than I was.

"I did all this in a very nonfeeling, nonpersonal way at first. But I began to wonder how this was, that I had this power and I was able to go back to the home office and say, 'Look, this guy needs to be removed,' and he gets sent back to the home office to a nine-to-five job with no future. When I'd see these guys buried someplace, back at the drafting board with a kind of downcast look about them, I began to ask myself what was going on.

"I began to wonder, considering all the inefficiencies I saw (padded expense accounts and people doing jobs that created other jobs that weren't needed in the first place) if the only mistake these guys had made was maybe not being good politicians, or possibly *refusing* to be politicians?

"Right in the middle of all this introspection I got into a situation where our priorities, which were supposed to be the security of the United States and maintaining a schedule and keeping the Air Force happy, could go sliding all over the place when our corporate image was threatened.

"We were getting ready to make a selloff to the Air Force on a system at Vandenberg, and we had to fire the missile successfully. Well, we punched a button and the goddamned thing blew up on the pad. The next thing we knew the place was swarming with security guards. Nobody could do anything. They brought in the fire people and put out the fire and the next three months I was on investigating boards that were supposed to find out why the thing blew up. What we really did was hassle about who was going to take the *blame* for this missile blowing up.

"It didn't really matter that there was a schedule to be met, which was *all* that mattered before. We just sat around the table saying things like, 'North American didn't have anything to do with it, our engines worked perfectly,' and Douglas Aircraft was saying, 'Our missile worked perfectly, it was a problem with North American's engines.' And the Air Force was saying, 'Jesus Christ, will somebody please tell us what's going on?'

"There was always tremendous pressure on us to maintain an image of perfection and supercompetence. Sometimes a missile contract was the only thing that was keeping the company going and the guy who messed up a contract or even looked like he was about to mess up one, was pulled back to the home office faster than the speed of light. And when that happened your career was over.

"There was a project manager for one of the subcontractors at Vandenberg. This guy came to Vandenberg happy, carefree, a nice friendly fellow, capable; the whole business. Nine months later, the poor son of a bitch was chainsmoking Robert Burns cigars. He was just about thirty-five and he'd come out of the meetings shaking like a leaf.

"I could no longer say to myself, 'Ho, ho, ho, that's not going to happen to me,' because it *was* happening to me too.

"I was getting an ulcer and I was on steroid pills because I was going through a big thing about not being able to digest any food. I'd been eating eight meals a day and losing five pounds a week.

"I'd been in the hospital four days and nobody could figure out what was wrong, but vaguely I saw some connection between this guy disintegrating and what was going on with me.

"After North American I thought I'd had enough experience as staff assistant to the manager of base activities. I was promoted to assistant manager at Forbes Air Force Base at Topeka, Kansas. Now so far as I was concerned, Topeka, Kansas, was nowheresville. It's hot in the summertime and the wind blows twenty-four hours a day, seven days a week, perpetually from the Saskatchewan border all the way to the Gulf Coast.

"I didn't want to go to Kansas but ended up going because it was the way to climb the ladder. I got to Kansas and there was no place to live. I wound up living in a trailer in the boondocks.

"There wasn't any real equipment. I had twenty people to keep busy and I didn't have anything to keep them busy with. We didn't have any missiles or equipment on site so on certain days I sent people fishing. There simply wasn't anything for them to do.

"I went there in May and this fooling around went on through summer and into fall. While I was there I made some decisions. I decided I needed to do something, but I wasn't sure what. But I knew I needed to get the hell out of Kansas.

"I realized I was unwilling to pay the price to climb the

ladder. I felt I was wasting myself and considered going back to school. So what I did was to apply at a bunch of graduate schools and also send out résumés to Boeing in Seattle and Lockheed in Palo Alto.

"Boeing wrote me a letter saying, 'Oh, boy! We want you. We want you. When can we come and see you?' Three days later I got a telegram from Boeing saying that, 'We have been notified by North American that you are unavailable. Thank you for your interest in Boeing.' I was sore as hell. So I called my boss and said, 'Hey, boss, I'm calling you for a particular reason.' And he said, 'Before you tell me what your reason is I want to tell you that we want you back at the home office as staff assistant to the division. You are to be on a plane tonight for a briefing tomorrow morning and be here full time in two weeks.'

"I said O.K., 'Maybe now I don't have to tell you I was calling to say maybe it's time for me to quit.'

"I went back to the home office. They had brought in a new executive and I was going to be his staff assistant.

"There were two ways to climb the ladder at North American. One was line management such as I was in at Forbes AFB. You're right in on what's going on and what's being done. The other was to be a staff assistant and just get higher and higher staff jobs. I preferred staff because on a staff job you're an advisor to a guy who has all the responsibility, and I preferred to let somebody else take all the grief.

"As a staff advisor I had a lot more freedom. I could come in late, leave early, and think up all kinds of reasons why I had to go out of town.

"As it happened, the guy I went to work for turned out to be an alcoholic and I spent most of my time covering up for him. For instance, we went to an out-of-town conference and got there in the afternoon. The meeting was supposed to start at 8 A.M. the next day, so this guy said he'd like to go out for a few drinks.

"What he did was to hit a few bars and ended up getting hung with some woman, getting in her Cadillac and not telling anyone where he was going. When the time came to show up the next morning, he wasn't there. I had to send off another supervisor with the story that my boss wasn't feeling well and would make it over as soon as he could.

"I was running all over the place trying to find out where he was, when he showed up looking sheepish and asking, 'Well, where are we?' I said, 'You're covered if you shave, put on a clean shirt, and get to the meeting,' which he did.

"In addition to feeling like a nursemaid, because of course this kind of thing happened more than just a few times, I began to have some really serious thoughts about putting ICBMs in silos all over the country.

"From the time I left Vandenberg I was a member of a team of Air Force contractor personnel who were on call any time an alert was on. *We* were the ones who were going to be responsible for manning the sites because at that time military personnel were incapable of manning the bird. *We* were going to end up in the blockhouse pushing the button.

"And regardless of what the politicians and the military were telling people then, our missiles weren't that accurate. It used to get to some of the other guys too and they'd go around telling people they met, 'We're working to put a man on the moon,' despite the fact that most of North American's business was coming from ICBMs.

"Well, the summer of 1961 an acceptance notice from the graduate school at San Jose State reached me. It had gone to Kansas and bounced around and finally got to me through the home office. I came home and found this thing in the mailbox and thought, 'Jesus Christ, a way out!'

"At that point, I really didn't have too much to think about. I'd made my decision little by little ever since I left Vandenberg. It was fortified in Topeka and fortified again when I was transferred back to the home office. The next day I went in and gave them my resignation. 'Well,' North American said, 'let us pay your way,' because they figured this was advanced scientific education. But I told them I didn't want them to pay my way, because I didn't want to be obligated. What they did do, though, was to put me on leave of absence without pay for the time I wanted to go to school.

"I had enough money saved, so finances were no problem, but I had a transition problem at San Jose State that I hadn't expected. The faculty knew I'd been out in the world, and I think they didn't know how to deal with me. They couldn't act with me like I was a kid, yet they were in a position of power over me, and they didn't want to give up that feeling so easily. The first year was like being in a fencing match. They'd win a bit and I'd win a bit. I was aware that it was turning out to be like the old corporate system, but I thought, 'What the hell, I'm getting what I want.'

"North American asked me to come back at the end of the first year. Another guy from Base Activation and I were put in charge of the maintenance engineering program. This group's purpose was to write maintenance manuals for Rocketdyne's engine systems and ground support systems. The thought in management's mind was that this function either needed to be cleaned up or eliminated, and it was our job to decide which.

"I went back in July and by December this other guy and I had decided maintenance engineering didn't need to exist and so we axed it. Well, this section involved over two hundred people so we scurried around and found jobs for most of them.

"After we'd axed maintenence engineering I was assigned to a job where I didn't have anything much to do. I was poor at making work, and better at eliminating jobs. I realized the thing to do was go back to school and finish my master's in oceanography, so I went back in the fall—again on leave of absence. And again North American wanted to pay my way, but I only let them pay for some books.

"My second year at San Jose State was a lot more comfortable for everybody. I was more committed, a fact that wasn't lost on the faculty. I still had the fantasy that I was going to be a research oceanographer for North American and I'd have a little lab and stay out of all that stuff I was into before. But I thought maybe one reason North American had been willing to pay my way at school was they thought I'd be willing to conform when I got back.

"Looking at the whole North American thing from the distance of San Jose State, I saw that going back into that place with an idea of having anything of myself left over was crazy.

"As long as you are part of the system, you are always expected to cover for someone, writing their report or making someone or the company look better than they really are, and I guess the payoff is money.

"The higher I got the less of my time was available to me. When I worked at the home office, I never lived in San Fernando Valley, near the company. I lived out in the mountains and I was not supposed to live there because my home was not available for entertainment. And I wouldn't go to very many of the parties—only when there were people I liked.

"But those parties were where the deals were negotiated. We spent time around a conference table, but if you missed the parties, you were dead. The system became important, and not the people in it. It became very impersonal. You could never let yourself get too friendly no matter who you dealt with, because tomorrow they might be expendable and if they were your friends, then you'd be in a box with them.

"Looking back on it now, I realized that it was only *after* I'd left North American for my second year at graduate school that I went through all the sorting out that really enabled me to quit the system. And what that says to me is that I was caught in the net a lot more than I realized.

"During my second year at San Jose State a lot of faculty pressure was on me to go on and get my Ph.D. San Jose State had to put so many master's in the Ph.D. pipeline to make a name for itself, but I said, 'I can beat that system. I'll apply for a grant and the competition's so great I won't get it and I can say, 'Well, I tried,' and I'm off the hook.' Well, that's what I did, except that I was offered a National Science Foundation grant to go on and get a Ph.D.

"So I packed my bags and sent my things to Tallahassee, Florida. Florida State was a southern school and southern schools have always been behind the eight ball.

They need to get high-powered grad students and a high-powered faculty that can produce paper after paper. It was like being back in the North American Aviation system, only I wasn't getting any money to go with it. It was produce, produce, produce.

"There was nothing much in Tallahassee except the southern conservative element and to some extent I found myself in cultural shock. When I got off the plane in Tallahassee it was like I'd been in a time machine and gone back thirty years. I put in my time at F.S.U. and went off to Antarctica on an expedition and when I came back took a short-term job with a consulting firm in Los Angeles.

"But it was like the aerospace industry all over again. The vice president I was working for had to have three martinis before lunch and he was dropping pills like they were going out of style. He had himself an $80,000 house in the Pacific Palisades, where he, his wife, and his children lived, except that I don't think he ever saw his wife.

"At this point I found myself in a quandary. I wanted the money, but at the same time I didn't fit the corporate mold anymore. I felt there was no place to go. I was running out of choices; I had tried the big industrial world and didn't seem to want that. I tried the educational world and sure as hell wasn't going to get into a publish-or-perish bind. The only thing I could do was finish my degree, so I went ahead methodically and did my research at F.S.U. I had married in Tallahassee, and my wife and I were soon in trouble with each other. I went to a psychologist and then talked her into going. He said, 'Hey, she needs some help,' so we went to a Georgia clinic where a guy said she needs some *real* help. Well,

I didn't want her driving back and forth to Georgia so she ended up getting a job that was near a Miami encounter group.

"She called me one day and said there was going to be a marathon encounter and to come down. We went, and it was great! I thought, maybe this is a way out of the whole mess!

"What happened was that I finally began to get in touch with who I was and where I wanted to go. My wife and I made a commitment that we would wait a year before we did anything. I think maybe if we'd got into this kind of thing sooner in our marriage or sooner as individuals before we met, we could have made it. But as it was, after a year we decided to split.

"Well, when I came down to Miami I saw this Miami-Dade County Junior College ad in the paper for an ocean-ographer, which I just happened to be, so I applied for the job and they offered it to me.

"I got the job against a lot of competition partly because I was local and they didn't have to spend a lot of money interviewing me or moving all my stuff. I took that job at Miami-Dade just to try it, never dreaming I'd enjoy teaching or be especially good at it. But it turned out I was a good teacher.

"The first year was a pretty neat thing. They had a free atmosphere at Miami-Dade and we were able to run our classes the way we wanted. The second year it changed. We got a new vice president, we had a cut in the budget and things became much more rigid. The new vice president started talking about not giving 'F's' and about getting kids through science courses who really couldn't get through them. His reasoning was that they were really trying to get through and couldn't afford to fail. I made some objections, but could see it was either play the game or get out, so I quit.

"Well, I had an opportunity to become a motivational therapist, working with a psychiatrist who had run some of the weekend encounters I'd gone to, so here I am. I'm back into my Ph. D. program, this time in psychology, and I'm comfortable with what I'm doing. I'm not making any money, and I'm beginning to find that money is time.

"If you have money you can afford to have your boat hauled instead of having to do it yourself. As a kid I'd worked a while as a carpenter, laid bricks, and there was a certain amount of satisfaction in it. But I don't enjoy doing it if I *have* to.

"So now I'm looking forward to the time when I've finished my Ph.D. and have more money, but I won't go back into the system to do it. I don't think I'll have to because I'll be able to work as a clinical psychologist with my own practice.

"Another good thing that's happened to me is that I've met the only woman I've ever felt like putting down roots with. We've been married just a few months, and even though neither one of us is making very much, I'm less concerned about money now than I have been for many years. Neither one of us cares very much about where we lay our heads so we don't mind the kind of place we have, no decorating it to suit our friends or any of that.

"Now that I'm in a relaxed unstructured way of life I'm beginning to see how much time it takes just to live. I worked so many hours a day and had to travel so much of the time, 'living' was no more than a pastime. We're all caught up in getting someplace and making money and the last thing we consider is a living pattern of doing what you want and being with people you want to be with.

"I guess for me the greatest thing about getting out of the system was doing something about my future instead of just falling into it."

.

7

David Youland: From Living on Maalox to Living in Maine

At thirty-four, David Youland resigned his $18,000 a year position as a middle-manager executive with United Parcel Service—but not to escape from a seemingly heartless or unappreciative corporation.

He liked the company he worked for, and UPS had responded to his outstanding performance by granting him frequent promotions that increased his salary from $4,000 to nearly $20,000 annually over a period of eight years.

David Youland gave up the security of his job, came home to work temporarily as a school bus driver, and mortgaged the house he and his wife had built with their own hands, because like Larry Murphy, Ralph Graham, and Bill Neeley, the demands of corporate life left him no time for the things that mattered most.

In hardly more than a year after quitting his job, David Youland and his family are living "the good life" operating their own hunting and fishing camp in Maine's remote north woods. Today he's running his camp's ad in *Field and Stream:*

BRADFORD CAMPS
MUNSUNGUN LAKE—AROOSTOOK RIVER HEADWATERS
Accessible only by float plane. Native Brook Trout, Lake Trout, Blueback Trout & Landlocked Salmon. 3 outpost camps—canoes on several other waters reached by air or trail. American plan—no hskpng. accommodations—individual party cabins with all conveniences. Hunting: Deer & Bear during Oct. & Nov. Open Jan., Feb. & Mar. for snowmobile parties by reservation. Write: David Youland, P. O. Portage, Maine 04768 • Winter: R. F. D. #1, Turner. Maine 04282 • Tel: 207-225-2587

Long before he was able to place that ad in *Field and Stream,* David Youland bought hunting and fishing magazines by the handful to read while waiting in lonely airport terminals and empty motel rooms as a traveling supervisor for UPS. He had time to reflect on what was happening to his life. "I found that I had certain goals in life, that they involved being with my family and working on our home and getting out in the woods. All things I couldn't do and continue my job with UPS."

In December of 1970, the pressures and conflicts of attempting to hang on to a life of his own while meeting his commitment to United Parcel, sent David Youland to the hospital with a bleeding ulcer.

"In October," he says, "after I'd just completed a four months' traveling assignment out of Boston as personnel manager for the 275 people we had in Maine and New Hampshire, I was assigned to manage driver and supervisor training in Philadelphia.

"During the mid-fifties we'd tried to open up there, but had to close down because of labor disputes and the unions fighting with each other. The company had decided that now was the time to go back and try again.

"We hired all new people for what had been a 1200-

man operation and I began training those people right in the middle of the Christmas rush. Our loads increased from 7,000 to 17,000 packages a night in a matter of weeks, which isn't very much in an area as big as Philadelphia. Soon we'd managed an increase of another 10,000 packages a night and cut an hour out of the day. We really had a sense of accomplishment.

"I was working from 10 P.M. until 9 A.M. and Nancy and I were trying to build our house, so I was on the phone all the time and worrying about an exposed foundation I had to get a roof over.

"I'd work all night Sunday night, Monday night, Tuesday night, Wednesday night, Thursday and Friday night and rush to get out of work a little early Saturday morning so I could catch the 7:15 A.M. flight to Portland, Maine.

"I'd land in Portland about 9:30 A.M. and Nancy would pick me up in the car. We'd get home about 11:30 and I'd work all day on the house. Of course I'd already lost a night's sleep. I'd get a little sleep Saturday night if I was lucky, and then work on the house all day Sunday. I'd leave home about 5 P.M. Sunday afternoon to catch the seven o'clock plane from Portland to Boston.

"There were about twenty minutes between the time my flight arrived in Boston and Northeast's flight for Philadelphia, so if the plane from Portland was a few minutes late, I'd literally have to run the whole length of Logan terminal to make my connection.

"Half the time I'd find the Philadelphia plane had been delayed or cancelled or oversold or something and I'd end up getting into Philadelphia about 11:30 at night, already an hour and a half late for work. And I'd work all night. I was getting five nights sleep each seven days.

"There were times during the Philadelphia assignment when I'd go back to my motel room and, God, double up with pain. Once I passed out from throwing up, but I tried to tell myself it was the flu. I was taking Maalox and tranquilizers and was resigned to the fact that I was going to live on that stuff. After a while I became almost immune to the pain in my stomach.

"One weekend right after Philadelphia, I was home and decided to go downtown and get some electric heaters. I was doing all the wiring myself and wanted to get those heaters in the new addition so we could use it. When I got home I felt pretty bad and had my wife call the doctor. He examined me and said I had a bleeding ulcer. If this wasn't a warning to me then nothing was, because what was happening was that I was bleeding to death."

As a kid, David Youland did the things most kids do; he was a Boy Scout and had a paper route and he says there's nothing special he remembers about his childhood, except maybe one thing which taught him that "some values have to come before your job."

"My father was a traveling passenger agent and had worked for the railroad for fifteen years. When I was about thirteen the railroad merged with another and they offered my dad a higher position in management if he would move to New York. He had been away a lot when I was growing up and when they asked him to go to New York he resigned and went to work for a machinery company where he stayed until he retired.

"I think my father's being away from home so much and the memory of how our family came alive when he quit the railroad, even though we had less money, were what prompted me to leave UPS.

"Even before my father quit the railroad I used to spend summers at my grandmother's farm a few miles west of Turner. I'd work on the farm and used to take out a .22 and hunt woodchucks. We had hunters and fishermen come on the farm sometimes and when I was old enough I'd go right along with them. I learned a lot about nature and the woods those summers and I think that's where I developed my love of the out-of-doors.

"After we got out of high school Nancy and I decided to get married and the jobs I had after that didn't leave me much time for hunting or fishing even though I was determined not to give up the outdoors any longer than I had to. Nancy and I figured it would be a good idea for me to go back to school, so we moved to Portland and I enrolled at the University of Maine.

"It was tough financially, and when Nancy became pregnant I left school and got a job in an orchard pruning trees and picking apples. It was 1958, and I was making $54 a week for fifty-four hours' work. When the baby came along I went to work for the Canteen vending-machine company as a driver. I worked for them three years and built up my territory until I was making more than a lot of drivers who'd been there much longer.

"When they cut back my route and gave parts of it to other drivers I quit and went to work for a machine company as tool-crib attendant. When I heard a rumor they were going to go out of business I started looking around for another job and learned that United Parcel Service was hiring drivers at $2.00 an hour.

"I drove for UPS three years and still might be driving for them if I'd been able to be with my family more and hunt and fish. But I was being torn between job security and doing what I wanted to do.

"After I'd been with UPS a few years, Nancy and I were better off financially than we'd ever been. If we wanted to go out for a steak Saturday night, we went. We didn't care if the bill was $20 or $40 we were out for a good time.

"When I became a supervisor I had eight drivers working under me. I managed the UPS operation at Auburn, Maine. A few months after I made supervisor, UPS extended its service throughout the state of Maine. In the meantime, the company had asked me to train drivers at Waterville, about fifty miles north of Auburn, and before long they also had me supervising drivers at Lewiston. In a very short period, I had gone from supervising eight drivers to twenty-two, which is enough work for about two-and-a-half men.

"I was handling it the best I could, but wasn't satisfied with the progress I was able to make, and wanted about eight extra hours in a day. Even so, the company asked me to take over Presque Isle, Maine, about 250 miles north of where I was working.

"So here I was. I was flying, I was driving, I was working fourteen or fifteen hours a day, yet I didn't have the satisfaction of making any progress because my responsibility was too vast for me to manage in any realistic way.

"UPS had a fairly exact sense of what it expected of each driver: he should be able to deliver so many packages and drive so many miles in so many hours and so on; but those calculations didn't seem to apply when it came to how many drivers or operations I had to supervise.

"In addition to the long hours, a couple of things were happening to me that I didn't feel too good about. When my promotion to supervisor came along I had to accept that when the company wanted me to be at point 'A' then that's where I had to be. I explained this to Nancy and said, 'we'll have to accept this.' In a way it was what I wanted: a sense of growth and respect and success.

"On the other hand, I didn't want the organization to rule my life and dictate what our future was going to be. It was like my ulcer. I ignored certain aspects of my new management status, the same way I tried to ignore the pain in my stomach.

"Another thing that changed when I became supervisor was that I was no longer the 'nice guy' the drivers worked *with* any more. I was the guy they had to watch out for: the boss.

"I tried to remain the person I was, but I had become a manager and I found it hard to supervise guys I once thought of as my buddies. Only after I left UPS did I reestablish some of these friendships."

Before David had been a supervisor for many months, Nancy Youland began to chafe under her new burdens. "With David away so much of the time I had to assume almost full responsibility for running the family. It's not that I felt there were things only David or I should do, it was just that there was too much for one person to handle."

With two young daughters, and another child on the way, Nancy and David felt the pressure mounting for him to spend more time at home, but those same responsibilities made them feel there was little they could do.

Nancy remembers, "I took care of paying the bills and keeping the checkbook and handled all our financial affairs. David deposited his paycheck and lived off his expense account. The rest was up to me. I was the only one home most of the time, and while maybe the girls need to share less time with their father than a boy, all the children needed a man's approach and way of seeing things that I just couldn't provide.

"Carrying all of that took a lot out of me and I felt the drain quite deeply, especially, I think, because David wasn't there to put anything back.

"There were times, just seconds here and there, when it was easy to forget there *was* a David. I caught myself making decisions and plans as though he weren't part of my life."

Though David accepted several assignments the company felt would 'round him out' for bigger things with UPS, he and Nancy had already begun to talk about what the job was doing to their lives and to consider what they could do to regain closeness with each other and the children.

David increased his efforts to get home as much as possible, and to be with his children on occasions that were especially important to them. But soon after his driver supervision responsibilities were back to near normal at Auburn, UPS gave David a new assignment, one the company regarded as a necessary building block in his career if UPS was to realize his full potential. He was sent to the company's Boston office, a five- or six-hour drive south of Turner, to learn something about personnel work.

David remembers what it was like, pushing himself to make it home several times a week. "I might leave Boston in the afternoon and drive five hours up to Turner because one of the children was in a school play or something and then turn around and drive five hours back to Boston to be there for work in the morning. I'd missed *all* the last year's plays and I was determined that this year I was going to be there.

"I felt strongly that my family was my first responsibility, but the reality was that I was giving top priority to my job. I was getting results, but I wasn't happy with the way my life was working out.

"I was traveling all over Maine and New Hampshire explaining company benefits to new employees and interviewing and hiring drivers. I'd set interviewing hours in Portland and Manchester and then if there was an opening in, say, Laconia, New Hampshire, I'd drive over there. There were days when I started out in Portland and interviewed people in two states before I checked into a motel three hundred miles from where I'd started the day.

"Somehow I struggled through that assignment. I didn't know anything about personnel work when I'd started so I really had to strain to learn it. I don't think personnel was my cup of tea at all. Then in October of 1970 I was reassigned to driver training, the Philadelphia assignment that produced my ulcer attack.

"I think what made it possible for me to see my way out from under all that pressure, and to live through that nine-week layoff getting over my ulcer, was a seemingly offhand thing that happened earlier that year when Nancy and I were on vacation in upper Maine.

"We'd been back in the woods in our camper, following some of the logging roads, when we came across a hunting and fishing camp and I said, 'Gee, I'd like to do something like that,' and Nancy said, 'Well, let's do it.'

"After our vacation was over and we got back to the routine, it never left my mind. As my job took me to different places I would talk to land owners, forest management companies, and newspapers to see what hunting and fishing camps might be available for purchase. I had several long talks with people at the Seven Islands

Land Company, a corporation that manages other people's land. After I got to know the people at Seven Islands, one of the men mentioned one or two places he thought might be available.

"One of the places was the Bradford Camps, on Munsungun Lake, north of Baxter State Park and about fifteen miles east of Chamberlain Lake. I wasn't especially interested in this particular camp, I thought maybe it was too remote, but I said 'O.K., we'll look at it.' Nancy and I drove up to Chamberlain Lake, but the weather was too bad to fly in, so we went back home.

"The next day I went up again and five minutes after we'd landed on the lake I said, 'This is it.' I'd made up my mind. This was in November and it took quite a few months to finally work everything out.

"Milt Hall and his wife, Mina, who were the owners, didn't want to sell to just anybody. They didn't want the camps to become just another resort and they wanted to make sure any new owner would maintain the place the way they had and that he'd have whatever it took to make it a success.

"In June, after I was in fairly good physical shape, a problem came up in the New Bedford, Massachusetts, office. The manager down there had something like fifteen girls working on billing and tracing and things weren't going well. The company asked me to fill in during the manager's vacation and to see what I could do to solve the problem there.

"Well, that was something I did not go for at all. I wanted to help that guy and not to undermine him. My dilemma was, should I lay out the problems before my boss or not? Strictly speaking, my responsibilities were to UPS and not to this manager. I really got muddled up by that and very cautiously tried to do the best I could without damaging this guy any more than I had to.

"The billing hadn't been out on time since the New Bedford office had been opened. The first week I was there we got the billing out a day early.

"I found those people were treated more like high school kids than adults. One of the fellows who ran the office would clap his hands like a schoolteacher if someone was talking. I knew I had to change this atmosphere.

"I outlined each person's responsibilities and explained what had to be done by the end of each week. I kept a close check on everyone's progress and if someone began to fall behind, I asked the person why. If they needed help, I gave it.

"I didn't manipulate these people. It was just a case of organization, letting people know what their responsibilities were. And I didn't clap my hands if people talked. As long as talking didn't disrupt the office I didn't see anything the matter with it.

"After I got the office running smoothly I requested a transfer. I asked myself where my career was at that point and I couldn't find an answer. I hadn't been satisfied with my New Bedford assignment even though I was satisfied with my accomplishment. In a matter of six weeks I had done things nobody had thought were possible. I had no idea of where I was going next.

"While I was in New Bedford I'd kept in touch with Milt and Mina Hall about purchasing the camps, had some correspondence and made some phone calls to lawyers and banks about what I was hoping to do. During the time I was in New Bedford I'd gotten some feedback from friends in the company to the effect that they'd heard I was dissatisfied and was leaving. I figured it was just a matter of time until my boss asked me about it, so I finally had to ask myself, 'Should I or shouldn't I do it?'

"I did have security on my job, and UPS had a good retirement program. I'd started with UPS at $80 a week and now, almost eight years later, my salary and stock incentive plan and other benefits came to about $18,000 a year.

"As far as performance was concerned, I'd adjusted well to management. I felt at the time that I could have been more of a success if I'd had a little more education, a little more refinement. I found it difficult at times to put my thoughts into words. So I didn't feel confident about how far I'd be able to go in the company.

"What I did know for sure was that I wasn't living the right kind of life for *me*. My ulcer told me that. And I didn't need anyone to tell me that it wasn't a very good deal for Nancy or the kids for me to be away all the time. She rarely complained, but if I'd have been in her place, it would have been easy to resent having to carry that responsibility by myself, and having a husband who was hardly ever home.

"Nancy and I were better off financially than we'd ever been, but when you start measuring success by material things in life, you miss the whole idea of life. Well, the minute those words came together in my head, my decision was made: I would resign.

"The next Friday night, after talking some things over with me at the office my boss said, 'You've got time, let's go out to dinner.' We stopped and had lobster and the whole thing and I said to myself, 'This has got to be it.'

"He said, 'Ah, I heard a rumor you're leaving,' and I said, 'As a matter of fact, it's true,' and I reached in my pocket and passed him my resignation. Then we discussed it for a while.

"Boy did I ever feel good when I left there! Quitting that job was the hardest thing I'd ever done in my life. The way I felt, Nancy and I had our whole life ahead of us. I was thirty-three at the time, and if I was going to do something different, now was the time to do it."

Nancy Youland knew her husband's resignation had awaited only the moment when he could talk with his boss. For nearly a year she and David had discussed every aspect of their adventure.

"I wasn't exactly looking forward to getting a job," she says, "but I knew that what David was doing, he was doing because he cared for us, because he felt there were more important things he could give us than money. With David home I had a husband again, and some of the things I couldn't do around the house, David would take care of when he was home between his morning and afternoon runs in the school bus.

"Actually, I didn't have much time when David quit to think about things anyway. He resigned his job on the fifteenth of July and we went up to the camps on the twentieth to start work for the summer so we'd get to know the place and learn as much as we could from Milt and Mina Hall.

"I worked with Mina in the kitchen and David worked with Milt on as many different jobs as he could. Before we were up there many weeks I could see quite a difference in David. His tension didn't build up overnight and I saw him beginning to un-wind. He could take more things in stride and wouldn't fly off the handle like he sometimes did when he was home from UPS.

"We were paid our value that summer and knew from the experience that we could manage anything that had to be done in connection with running the camps. The kids loved the place and had their father back, so it was a good summer for them.

"I felt that if we could make ends meet through the winter, and if David could get the financing we'd need, and if we could get enough guests lined up for the next season, we'd make it."

David and Nancy returned to Turner in time to get the children enrolled in school, and see to their financial needs: a job for himself, a job for Nancy, and financing for the camps. Milt and Mina Hall had offered terms, and Milt had agreed to stay on at least through the first season as one of the camp's four guides.

Nancy went to work packing apples, wrapping individual apples in purple tissue, filling crates for shipment throughout the Northeast. "They paid piecework," Nancy said, "and I was pretty fast, so I could count on bringing home enough each week to pay the grocery bill."

David began working in a resort ski shop near Turner. "One morning after I was there a few weeks, I went in and opened up and was the only one there. I found some rental skis that needed repair and started working on them. About 9:30, the three other guys sauntered in, half an hour late. Well, these fellows were sitting around talking and I'm the only one working, when the fellow doing the payroll upstairs comes down and says, 'We don't need you today.' Me, the only one working.

"Well, I was the newest, so in a way I could understand, but I said, 'If you don't need me, why didn't you call me so I wouldn't have had to drive down?' and he told me, 'It's not our task to call you, if you want to know, you should phone us.' So I told him, 'If that's the way you feel, why don't you just mail my check,' and I walked right out the door. I was feeling pretty independent, being able to do that.

"When Nancy came home I was sitting on the couch and she asked me, 'What are you doing home?' I told her I'd quit. 'You quit!' she shouted at me. 'How could you? It was the only job you had,' and she was going through the house shouting at me and so on for a while.

"The school district had been after me to drive the school bus in town, but for less money than the ski shop paid, and since I was thinking mostly about money when I'd come back in the fall, I took the other job. Now the school bus job looked pretty good, so I was driving the bus by the end of the week.

"It was a good deal for me because it left me the main part of the day to go after financing and handle all my correspondence.

"The day I started after financing I didn't think it would be too difficult. I had my house and a record of always paying my bills. A friend at the commercial bank where we had our account suggested I see a savings bank, because they have lower interest rates. I went to several savings banks, but those people weren't interested in doing business with me because I didn't have a job. I showed them income projections for the camps, but they weren't interested in that. All they wanted to know was, what was my monthly income?

"I told them, 'Look, I'm not going to put my house on the block unless I have a pretty good indication that I'll be able to meet my commitments,' but they just weren't willing unless I had a regular salary. I finally went back to the commercial bank we'd done business with for fifteen years and even they were hesitant. . . .

"Well, after I talked with the banker several times he

said, "We'll give you five thousand dollars on your signature. How much more do you need?' I told him and he replied that he didn't see any problem and would take a look at my house. Well, they sent a man out and he drove up the road and took a Polaroid picture. The same day the banker phoned and said, 'O.K., you've got your money.'

"I think the bank's decision was based mainly on my record with them over fifteen years. It would have been *very* difficult if I'd transferred around a lot with the family and had done business for short periods with several different banks. I had never been late with a payment in *fifteen years* with that bank.

"I remember one savings bank I went into, the fellow was talking about the camps and said he'd been there. It didn't sound right for some reason so I asked him, 'How long ago were you there?' and he said 'Forty-five years ago.' Jesus! He was going to base his evaluation of the camps on what he'd seen when he was a fourteen-year-old kid!

"Well I'd shown him my income projections and the previous owner's tax returns for the past three years, plus a long list of perfect credit references, but when I walked out of there I knew I was going to be turned down.

"It was a relief when my bank finally came through, because I'd already committed myself to buy the camps. Another thing I'd done when I committed myself to buy the camps was to start advertising. I took out an ad in *Field and Stream* and some of the New England hunting and fishing publications.

"I'd get back from my morning school bus run about 10 A.M. and do correspondence and legal things. About noon the mailman would come and I'd get maybe six letters in response to my ads.

"With both Nancy and me working we made it through the winter and toward the end of April I figured I'd better get up to Munsungun and take a look at the camps. We landed a ski plane on the lake and even that late in the spring snow was so deep I could walk over the roofs of the cabins on snowshoes.

"The winter of 1971 had been the coldest since 1932. There was so much snow, and there was so much ice still on the lake, that we had to cancel some of the early guests' reservations for mid-May. We had to make paths, backing the tractor in reverse, so we'd be able to get around."

The camps are located on the northeast shore of Munsungun Lake, about sevety miles northeast of Greenville, Maine.

"We're on land managed by the Seven Islands Land Company, a corporation which operates over a million and a half acres in Maine, mostly for multiple-use forest management. Ours is the only camp in the area so we have thousands of acres pretty much to ourselves. Most of the buildings—eight guest cabins, the main lodge, and three or four other cabins for the guides—were built around 1900. They're made out of ten inch logs, notched and crossed at the cabins' four corners just like the Lincoln log sets kids play with.

"Each cabin has a complete bathroom with hot water shower, gas lights, and a wood burning heater. Some cabins have two bedrooms and can sleep four to six people.

"The main lodge is three rooms, a big lounge, I guess you'd call it, that has a stone fireplace and some chairs, a dining room where we can serve twenty-four people at once, and the kitchen. Nancy does the cooking on two stoves, a gas stove and a big wood burning stove we use as much as we can, since we've got more wood than gas. All the gas cylinders come in by plane, two cylinders to a load, so we tend to go easy on the gas.

"Out behind the kitchen there's an ice house seventy-five years old. We come up here during the winter and cut ice right out of the lake and store enough to last out the summer. The water in the lake is pure, you can drink it any time.

"One thing we get plenty of compliments on is our food. Everything is fresh. We fly in seedlings for our garden when we need to, to get an early start on some vegetables, so all summer long we're growing corn, cabbage, green peppers, carrots, asparagus, beets, turnips, tomatoes, lettuce, broccoli, strawberries and raspberries. We also get apples from our own trees for pie. Any time you have vegetables at our camps, they were in the garden an hour ago. We fly in meat, but don't try to have milk because we're limited on refrigeration.

"We operate the camp almost exactly as it was run fifty years ago. We've got three outpost camps on the other lakes, with plenty of native brook trout, lake trout, blueback trout, and landlocked salmon on all the lakes. There's no fishing pressure on the lakes so no stocking is required.

"The whole thing more than lives up to what we hoped it would be," reports David in September, 1972. "The whole family was up here. We all worked together and enjoyed it so much it didn't seem like work. I think after we learn a bit we'll have more time off—after all how much living can you do when you get up at 5:30 A.M. and go to bed at 9:00 P.M., unless you enjoy your work?

"A lot of credit has to go to Milt Hall. Milt was always here so if a problem came up, like with the equipment or something, he showed us what to do. He worked as one of the guides and just having him around gave us a lot of confidence.

"Nancy and our teen-aged daughter, Kimberly, ran the kitchen alone until we could add someone else. Our son, Kurt, kept the outboards and canoes in shape, just like he'd maintained our snowmobiles at home. Nancy and I can see our way clear now to making a go of the camps, doing this thing together, and the experiences the kids are sharing are better than anything an expensive private school could offer.

"When Nancy and I came up here to work that first summer, I really was a novice with a canoe. They gave me a canoe and I went up to what they call the thoroughfare, a channel that runs between the north end of Munsungun Lake and Chase Lake. Well, I went up through it and back down and right back up again until I'd mastered it. I was going up and down that thoroughfare all summer.

"Several times after I'd got pretty good, I went up again when the water was a little fast—right after a storm—so it would be a little of a challenge. It was awfully easy to say, 'I don't think I'll go up there this time,' but I went up there anyway.

"I just got my private pilot's license, I'd learned to fly along with everything else last winter, and it was a lot like that canoe. If you let it get ahead of you, you can't say to yourself, 'Well, I think I'll just stop and think that through again.' You're moving all the time so you can't lose touch with the consequences of what you're doing.

"I think life is like that. You're moving all the time and if you don't take control you arrive at the end of it without having anything to say about it."

David Youland believes he'll probably get a temporary job again after he closes down the camp for the winter. But he doesn't see any need for Nancy to work and from next year on he feels they'll have time to travel together during their five months' vacation in the small plane he plans to buy at Christmas.

I asked David if there was anything about his new life that was a minus, something he didn't expect that might have tarnished the luster of his freedom just a bit. "Being away from Nancy a month or so in the spring and again in the fall," he said. "That's the only thing I can think of." How was his ulcer getting along? "What ulcer?" he laughed as he got up from where we'd been sitting in the sun on the lodge's front steps and walked down to meet a load of guests that had just arrived in a bright yellow Folsom's Air Service float plane.

8

Bob Cromey: A More Personal Kind of Ministry

Bob Cromey was an executive in one of the biggest organizations of them all. An ordained priest in the Episcopal Church, he'd risen from rector of an obscure New York parish to become number one assistant to one of the most widely known, and most controversial, churchmen in America, San Francisco's Bishop James Pike.

Bob Cromey was doing well in the ecclesiastical rat race and feels that had he not been guilty of rocking the boat he would be among the higher members of the church hierarchy today. "I was always popular as a minister. People sought me out and asked my advice and every weekend my wife and I were invited to two or three dinner parties. I got along very well with Bishop Pike, and my concern with the role of religious institutions and with liturgical reform, modernizing the conduct of the religious service, sustained my interest in the church."

"A friend who was working up the ladder at the same level I was when I left is now dean of a cathedral in the

East. I'm sure if I had kept my nose clean today, at forty-one, I'd be the dean of a cathedral or rector of a very large Episcopal parish in a suburb of a large city.

"But I became very discouraged about the Church, and had to step outside to fulfill my ministry.

"As a minister of the church it was all right to *talk* about the inequities being faced by minorities, blacks, and homosexuals, and it was O.K. to say, 'Christians ought to be concerned about the plight of black people,' for example. But it definitely wasn't O.K., at least as it seemed to me, to *do* anything about it.

"Well, I walked on picket lines and I marched in the streets; I was arrested. In 1964 I was elected to the Board of the San Francisco NAACP. I also criticized the church hierarchy for belonging to clubs that excluded memberships by blacks and Jews. I even helped find an organization to minister to homosexuals.

"I was criticized for 'dragging the good name of the church in the streets,' and I said, 'Look, we clergymen have to decide who we're going to please. Are we going to work with the blacks in the community and the poor people we're supposed to be involved with, or are we going to please the white establishment Episcopalians?'

"I made the choice that I was going to work with the minority portion of the community. The rest of the Episcopal Church would take care of the others anyway."

Like many administrators, Cromey was interested in "internal management," and in his case that included the liturgy of his church. "In addition to social issues I was also interested in liturgical reform, how to run church services, how to make them more beautiful and meaningful. I wanted to make the communion service, particularly, a spiritual experience. To me it was always boring.

It was called the celebration of Holy Communion, but it was about as joyful as going to a funeral.

"I was vicar of a parish for six years after I left full-time work in Bishop Pike's office and tried to make the communion service a great celebrative event. We had balloons and beautiful vestments. We used incense, not because it was spiritual, but because it smelled good. It was fun to play with incense.

"I tried to create a sense of real joy in people coming together to eat the bread and drink the wine in memory of Christ. We also did a lot of things with the kids, processions and parades around the church, keeping them involved actively, having them do things rather than just teaching them words.

"The kids came to the first part of the service where they were full, active participants. We didn't thin out the service to make it for the kids. That the kids were actively involved in *doing* something, instead of just saying something, meant they were learning by experiential participation. I think it worked very well. The kids felt at home in the church. They felt they could get up and walk across the aisle or up around the altar or around somebody's feet when they were singing. Nobody minded. In fact everybody thought it was kind of nice.

"But all along there was a lot of pressure to muzzle me. Conservative clergymen around the cathedral were saying to Bishop Pike, 'Here is Cromey, one of your executive assistants, always involving himself with trouble in the streets. Every time his name is mentioned, *your* name is mentioned. One of the reasons he gets so much publicity is because he's using your name to do it. . . .'

"But Pike was always very supportive and would say, 'Well, you're a priest of the Church, but you're no different from anybody else. If this is morally right for you, then you should do it, even though there is a risk for the bishop that I have to bear.' He was very supportive of my right to get arrested, even though he, himself, wouldn't go out and do it. I offered to resign a couple of times and he said, 'Absolutely not, it's troublesome, but we'll get through it.' I was beginning to understand the position that Bishop Pike, and the Church, were in, that it might be fairer to them, and better for me, if I were outside.

"Yet at this point I wanted to stay in the Church. I was married. I had children. I had an income. It wasn't much, but it was there every month. At that time there was an aspect of self-righteousness in my staying there. 'All right, Church, you come along with me because I'm on the right path.' Now I'm a little embarrassed about feeling like that, but it was there.

"One of my jobs as executive assistant to Bishop Pike was to screen the people who wanted to see him. One day Michael Murphy, one of the cofounders of Esalen, chief resource of the human potential movement, came to see Bishop Pike and said that he thought Bishop Pike would be very interested in what Esalen was up to. I said I thought Pike would be too, so we were both invited down to Esalen at Big Sur for a weekend.

"Bishop Pike led a workshop and I just participated. We both got interested in the human-potential thing so I started going down there regularly, getting involved in encounter and Gestalt and the other things. I saw what I thought was an obvious relationship between what the Church was *supposed* to be doing, and what the human-potential movement really *was* doing.

"Religions are great proclaimers of new life, joy, celebration, especially Judaism and Christianity, which I knew something about. The Church *talks* about these things, about forgiveness and love, about community and life, but it's the human-potential movement that has found ways to bring these experiences into people's lives. The Church talks about prayer and meditation, but the human-potential movement has taught people how to meditate.

"To me encounter equals confession and forgiveness in that when you're in an encounter group and you *really* tell everyone what you feel, it's like making your confession. You get all that out. After you've gotten rid of it, you feel forgiven. You feel good. That is what happens in a *good* encounter session.

"In a Church setting you go to confession and the priest says, 'You're forgiven,' but you walk out still *feeling* guilty. You don't *feel* forgiven. You've got a 'you are forgiven' stamp on your forehead, but it didn't really happen, didn't *experientially* happen.

"The Church has the laying on of the hands—'You're saved,' and all that—the human-potential movement has massage. But we actually *touch* people; we don't just put one finger on them and that's it. It's a really warm, affectionate, body contact, real caring.

"I think what grabbed me most though, about my experiences at Esalen, was Bill Shutz's emphasis and real push to get us to be open and honest. I found that as a clergyman so much of what I'd been doing was closed and dishonest. As a churchman, for example, it wasn't 'good' for me to get angry. Clergymen don't get angry, Bob Cromey doesn't get angry, and so on. Of course the guilt about being angry, and the anger itself, had always been held, tied up inside me.

"During one of the first fights my wife and I had, she

threw something at me across the room and I was just furious. 'Don't ever do that again,' I said with no emotion. What I was saying was, 'The only emotion I want from you is love and affection and lust, but don't be angry with me.' I think any good relationship has to be a lot wider.

"Now I'm always telling people in encounter groups to be regular Polish housewives, you know, really throw pots and pans and yell and scream and get that shit out and then sit down and talk about it. But don't sit down and try to talk about it when you're repressing all that. When all this heavy emotion is released in a straightforward and honest way you can talk, but until that happens, it's going to be tight.

"Of course when people lock up one kind of emotion, like anger, then the other things like affection and joy and spontaneity get blocked up. So we spend a lot of time getting those things out in the open too, although what you usually hear about encounter is the anger and resentment that comes out.

"In my earlier days as a minister, when people brought me problems, particularly problems of being sexually attracted to people outside their marriage, I was unprepared to help them in any significant way.

"When this same thing happened to me in the seminary, when I was troubled by being attracted to some of the other seminarians' wives, I went to the dean or the chaplain and they would say, 'These things come and they go, don't worry about it.' Their answer to these problems, and I think the answer of the Church generally, is 'Have Jesus as the center of your life,' or to say, 'We will kneel together and take it to God in prayer.'

"After a while I felt the whole idea of being dependent on God or Jesus Christ or the traditional formula just didn't make sense to me. They were formulae that I could understand intellectually, but they didn't work.

"Now, after having gone down to Esalen with Bishop Pike, I felt I was discovering something that *would* help me, and that would be a great deal more useful in helping people deal with themselves, than the traditional seminary-taught things I'd been given as approved tools for use in dealing with personal crisis.

"I was a high-school athlete—six feet four inches, heavy enough, all of that—and played all the team sports, baseball, football, basketball. But even though I was in a team sport, I was always more interested in how I looked, how I felt, than how I performed. I liked to win, of course, but I talked more about being a team man than I actually was. I liked being a star.

"I'm really very grateful to my mother and father. I never had any sense of being pressured by them into doing anything. My father was a clergyman also, and if anything, he discouraged me in that direction. He would say, 'Well, really think about lots of other things before you think about the ministry. Do that last.' And yet I think he was relatively happy as a clergyman.

"As for as my father is concerned, I suppose the one thing I wanted was for him to be a little more present with me, more focused on me. I remember once he got beaten up, and oh, he was a mess, bloody, black eyes, the whole thing, and he just would never say what had happened to him. I was in college at the time, and I remember thinking, 'Gosh, I feel bad that he doesn't trust me more.'

"I wanted my parents to demand more of me, rather than the opposite. I wish, for example, that they had pressed me a bit more toward doing cultural things.

"I remember wanting to be liked a lot, really wanting

other kids' affection, and yet never asking for it. In some ways, because I was very clever with my mouth and a smart ass, I would alienate people—when what I really wanted to do was draw them closer to me. And I find that the bullshit talk and teasing and laughing would be ways of keeping people away from me rather than drawing them to me. I wanted them close to me, but I think I looked at it as a weakness to ask for someone to be close.

"It was like that with my father. What I wanted from him was closeness, more closeness, but he kept his distance. He had a bit of a thing about being manly, being a man and not being a sissy, and I remember that as something he laid on me. My father was a great giver. He never asked for anything and never got anything, and then I think he grew resentful in his later days. And I eventually found myself in that pattern of always being available to people in need, and then growing resentful of them, of their impinging on my time.

"My early pattern was definitely 'do for others,' and it wasn't until I went to Esalen and got involved in some Gestalt things that I was able to say, honestly, 'I want things for myself,' and that it was O.K. to want things for myself. It was not quite right to do that in my family. My father's interests were always much more in doing for others. That was 'the right thing to do.'

"My father was a great collector of people with problems. His early parishes in Brooklyn were filled with troubled people, which is perhaps where my social conscience came from. There was a guy named Frank Mallerba, an Italian-American, and a family by the name of Pacino that was Philipine, and Louie Estalt and his family, Puerto Ricans. And these people were around my house all the time it seemed, because they were young and had trouble getting on relief and welfare, and some had left home because of family or girlfriend problems. So they were around when I was nine, ten, eleven, around there, and it was exciting and interesting, and certainly very different from the WASP people that my folks were.

"I have great memories of things like Frank Mallerba teaching us kids to swim, and some black people who stayed with us for a while, and all of these people were so much more fun than my relatives, for example, because they were open and free and you didn't have to behave in a certain way with them. So much of their life seemed to be based on 'What are you feeling? Do it.' and even when they would yell and argue, that was O.K. too, that was the name of the game. But not in my family or with my relatives.

"I feel now that I suffered a loss of freedom by going into the church. Deciding to be a clergyman closed me off forever from looking realistically at what business might be like, or newspaper writing, the whole idea of media which I was always interested in, fascinated by, but, 'Oh well, that's not for me,' I'd say. 'I'm going to be a minister.' Being a people helper really felt good, but it also kept me from those areas which were not specifically people-helping, anything that had pleasure in it. Like it might be fun to be on stage, to be an actor, but that was people-pleasing on a superficial level—people-pleasing rather than people-helping. So I limited myself in lots of ways.

"Once I realized that I was not going to be a professional athlete, what emerged was being a clergyman, being a social worker, or a teacher. Having been exposed to, in some ways, the best of church life at the time, nonpietistic, socially oriented, realistic, liturgical in that there were lovely services that seemed to move me psychically and spiritually—all those things I liked very much, so by the time I was a junior in college I was pretty certain I wanted to be a clergyman. That seemed to be big. And it followed my father's profession. He was a people-helper, and that seemed to me to be an interesting way to live. I had a head trip which said that was what God intended me to do, and it seemed like interesting work, fun work.

"And also it had a certain amount of built-in prominence, a certain amount of leadership in the community. I had that as a minister. As I look back, the last couple of years it turned to ashes in my mouth, but it was prominence of a sort. So being a clergyman came out of those mixed motives and of course in the early 50s we were very heavy, beginning the very strong influence on equality for black people, and that seemed right to me, being born and bred in Brooklyn and New York City where black people were just people I knew. I didn't have anything special about black people though I know I have deep kind of racist things in me, but certainly on the intellectual level it was the right thing to do to get involved in that and the ministry was a way to do that.

"I think awareness of my own sexuality is a very powerful part of my life and existence. I desired women outside my marriage and that made me doubt whether I was deeply religious. Why couldn't I be like other people and why did I have to have these desires when other people didn't seem to? And yet rationally and intellectually I thought 'Well, wherever there is love, wherever there is affection, it's the presence of God.'

"When I was making love with somebody else's wife, being married myself at the time didn't seem to matter.

But I was still being unfaithful, disloyal, adulterous, and all the rest. Even though my head said, 'Well, we have love, and I also have love with this lovely woman,' there were still a lot of questions raised that offended my own deepest sensibilities.

"But I went ahead and did it anyway, because I had some sense of needing and wanting more out of my own sexuality than I was getting in my marriage, or I thought I was getting in my marriage. I think sexuality had a lot to do with my being less pious, less needful of religion. Somehow it helped me be much more aware of my own body, my own emotions, my being willing to say, 'Look, these are real things. They're emotional and they're irrational.' It was the first time I really had to give in to my emotions, and give in to irrationality, give in to some other way of being, or knowing, rather than just saying I have to fit it into some category intellectually in order for it to be right. These things were right, but they weren't fitting into the categories, so I was in pain and felt guilt and anxiety.

"As a teen-ager I used to go to dances at a private girls' school and I remember being turned on to one particular girl. She was very beautiful, and I really liked her and I had a sense of her liking me. I used to hold her hand but I would never kiss her. I would never in any way get any closer physically; it was a great strain. I came up with a rationalization: well, my father was a clergyman and this was a church school, therefore I don't want to disgrace my father, therefore I won't kiss this girl. My reason took over; my reason said you mustn't let your emotions take over because you'll disgrace your father. I was afraid of my sexuality, obviously, and blamed my poor old man for it.

"I was a virgin when I got married at twenty-one. I had

been aroused by a number of women but it seemed right to be virgins when we got married . . . my wife and I were. But the moral thing was what held us back. It was morally right to wait.

"As a young minister, I found myself attracted to women and for many, many years I didn't do anything about it. In my first parish, I remember this happening. I still don't think you should commit adultery. I really believe the old commandment. However, I don't regard any of the precepts in the Bible as absolutes. Individuals, I think, have a right to make decisions on their own.

"Since I had been bothered by emotions—my feelings for other students' wives and so on—I decided in school that I would be intellectual and rational and that anything that was *emotional* wasn't important. So I tried to strain all the emotion out of my life.

"For me 'sex' meant a loss of freedom. I wasn't doing much acting out, some necking and petting when I was in high school and college. But it was very frustrating because I'd made the *rational* choice not to fool around. I had a lot of anxiety and worry about sex.

"One reason I became so promiscuous when I got to be thirty was that it was a way of handling the anger I felt toward my wife. It was also a way of saying, 'Man, I missed my adolescence.'

"I had been with another woman once before coming to California, but it was out here that I began playing around, being *involved* with other women. I had a sense of 'I don't care what happens, I'm going this route. I feel excited and I feel happy and I'm willing to take the consequences.' I felt anxiety that I was married and I had children, but my pietistic, my rational approach, hadn't helped and, so far as my unhappiness was concerned, this *worked.*

"When I went to social-action meetings women would be there and we'd go out to lunch and talk and intimacy began to develop. I became open to the idea of sexual intimacy and became involved with one woman for rather a long time and branched out from there.

"I think if my wife and I had been in a situation where we could be open with each other and deal effectively with what was going on there would have been enough in our relationship and our children that we would still have been together. But she found my promiscuity very hard to bear. . . .

"We were divorced several years ago. After I'd got into the human-potential movement I told Bishop Pike that I was tired of answering letters and so on and asked for assignment to a parish. I became vicar of St. Aden's Church in San Francisco and served there six years. It was during my last year there my wife and I were divorced. She moved East with the children and I stayed on at St. Aden's for six months.

"I was embarrassed about my sex life and my divorce and it seemed the best thing to leave and let the Church go its way and I'd go mine, which I did in early 1970. A lot of people got the idea that because I was a radical or got divorced I was expelled. But it was my own decision to leave. The Church gave me three months' severance pay and a room in the rectory rent-free for five months.

"One of the biggest anxieties I had about getting out was that I would not be able to make enough money. All my life I'd had a modest income from the Church and it was there every month. Suddenly I was confronted with the fact that *I* had to earn any money that came my way, and that was scary.

"I set a goal for myself of a thousand dollars a month, approximately what I was earning as a clergyman. And

I found that by leading a few groups and teaching massage and beginning my work with Esalen that I was making twelve, fourteen hundred a month without any trouble.

"I'd get up every morning and I'd work at being unemployed and try to figure out what to do next. When everything ran out with the Church I moved into the flat I'm in right now. I had two roommates and I was only paying $125 a month rent.

"I began to do more and more groups and then I worked part-time for the Esalen San Francisco office doing some administration. The fall of '70 I worked for the John Tunney for Senator campaign for three months. When the Tunney campaign was over in November of '70 I realized that I could earn my way quite well not having to do anything more than just lead groups. So I made the commitment to do that full-time. There was never a moment when I felt absolutely terrified or down in the dumps about income. It just evolved very, very naturally.

"I found that I spent some time cleaning the house— my desk and my environment had to be fairly organized so that I could function. I found that I liked working with my hands, doing the dishes and mopping the floor. In some ways, I regretted that I hadn't enjoyed that more when I was married."

The San Francisco air is cleaner than in many cities, so Bob Cromey and other San Franciscans ride bikes more than people do in other places. "I have a ten-speed bike which I ride as many places as I can. I ride some for pleasure every day, and I use it to go to my girlfriend's and to the store and the bank and places like that. I don't have an image to think about now like when I was in

Bishop Pike's office. I can be more free about things like bike riding.

"I have a white bike and a really bright red jumpsuit which keeps me warm and less likely to be run into, but I think it looks rather nice, too, in the bright green of the park, or with the darker colors of the buildings along the street; kind of a joyous thing to see—like a bright red balloon.

"Your body, your feelings, and your emotions are ways of knowing, just as your intellect is a way of knowing. Feelings are valid ways of knowing yourself and other people, knowing where you're at with yourself and the world. How many people ever stop to ask themselves, 'How am I feeling right now?' The answer can tell you a lot.

"One of my major satisfactions in life free of the Church role and traditional model of therapist-patient relationships is the freedom from the kind of situation where there's an overlay that presumes someone is 'sick.' Although I'm licensed as a marriage and family counselor, I consider my work with people much more in the line of growth and education than therapy.

"I could have done things differently than I have in my life, perhaps 'better' in someone's judgment, but I don't have a sense of 'if only.' I really don't. I take responsibility for my own life.

"What happens to me now is surely influenced by the past: but what's happening to me now involves choices of my own making. If I'm not happy about what's happening with my life I'm the only one who can do anything about it.

"The freedom to be 'me,' now that I'm responsible for my own actions, rather than, say, my role as a churchman being responsible for what I say and do, is a great joy. But my greatest joy is my personal relationship with the *one* woman in my life. I've gone full circle, from a monogamous marriage to promiscuity right back to the desire for a close, intimate relationship with one woman.

"In this relationship I've found the most joy I've experienced in a long time—fun, gay laughter, a great kind of celebrated sexuality. She has children and I think, if we were living together, I'd be more attentive to those children than I was able to be with my own.

"What has happened with me is that in getting out, what I took myself through to get out has changed the *quality* of time I have with people and the relationship I have with myself. I couldn't have found those things as I see it, by seeking them within the Church framework."

9

Breaking Free

Getting out of the rat race is more than changing careers, moving to a different part of the country or trading a business suit for blue jeans. Getting out requires that we develop an ability to choose our own actions and values.

We are used to talking bravely about what we *should* want in life, but are rarely so clear about exactly what we *do* want. Depending upon how closely tied we are to the values of the larger corporate world, we may choose our actions on the basis of how we think they will be accepted —rather than because of their intrinsic value. We may allay anxiety by working toward social acceptance.

Psychologist Carl Rogers points out that, "as an individual moves gradually toward a new type of realization, he experiences a dawning recognition that, in some sense, he chooses himself. He begins to realize that, 'I am not compelled to be simply the creation of others, molded to their expectations, shaped by their demands. I am increasingly the architect of myself.' " It is this consciousness of self that expands our control of our lives.

Americans are beginning to ask themselves, "Who am I? How can I get in touch with my real self and how can I become that person?" For people who have broken free of the rat race, the answers have come through moving away from what they are *not,* by no longer trying to live up to what they *ought* to be, by moving away from what society *expects* them to be and by no longer trying to live in a particular way just to *please others.*

Gradually these individuals are able to choose goals toward which they want to move. They learn to trust their own experience and values and they rely less and less upon what they perceive to be the judgment of society, the familiar assumptions of a well integrated materialist system.

Carl Rogers says that in learning to trust our own inner feelings we're able to communicate with the experience of being and the experience of feeling. "We learn to listen to ourselves and we can hear the messages and meanings being communicated by our own 'gut' reactions. When we're no longer fearful of what we may find we come closer to our own inner sources of information, rather than closing them off."

"Why is it," asks Erich Fromm, "that having everything for which one could wish, we are unhappy, lonely, and anxious? Is there something in our way of life, in the structure or value system of society, which is wrong? Are there other alternatives?"

Breaking free always involves conflict. Parents often feel they are losing control. Spouses fear they will be "outgrown." Employers fear eroding motivation of the worker and the corporate state is afraid that its markets and labor pools will be disrupted.

Let a man tell his employer that he really enjoys his work at the drafting board and doesn't want to be a manager, or let almost any corporate administrator tell his boss he doesn't want to "move up" and watch what happens. In the eyes of the company he becomes "lazy," has "no ambition," and "lacks confidence in himself." The company has no way of compensating a man who doesn't want to "get ahead" and finds it impossible to believe that anyone would work for the enjoyment of it. Such a man has rejected the values of his superiors and soon the fault-finding initiated by his honesty leads to his dismissal. Quite aside from the price such a man pays for his honesty, his company has lost the services of an individual who sets for himself the high standards of a man who loves his work.

To Yale University Law School's Charles Reich and psychiatrist Dr. David Viscott, the corporate state's fear of man finding his own values is very real. "The Corporate State," says Reich in *The Greening of America,* "runs by means of a willing producer who desires status, and a willing consumer, who desires what the corporate state makes him want." If men discover their own values and work toward their own goals, the corporate state, Reich says, "can no longer sell people things to satisfy anything but real needs. It can no longer get anyone to work except for real values."

"Society," writes psychiatrist Dr. David Viscott in his book *Feel Free,* "fears a free man. Whenever society sees someone who is truly free, it feels compelled to bind him up again. The person is branded as an outcast and categorized as odd and unconforming. Society must do this, because, by definition, society is an arrangement of rules to be conformed to. Not to conform is not to belong to society.

"A person who is truly free to follow the dictates of his own conscience and heart threatens that part of society [Reich's Corporate State], which depends on reliable productivity and consumption. The entire distribution of labor may be upset."

The threat experienced by the spouse of someone who is moving toward self-awareness is much the same as the threat experienced by the husband or wife whose partner enters psychotherapy. When one partner in a marriage moves toward making decisions free of society's value system, and becomes less concerned about what people will say or think, it is sometimes painfully obvious to husband and wife that one of them has changed in some fundamental way.

"When you decide to change," says psychiatrist Viscott, "your spouse is going to be threatened as nothing before in your marriage has threatened her or him. A real threat is either that a change *will* take place in the other that will allow him to stand on his own two feet, or that changes will force the other spouse also to make changes. To accommodate change, a spouse may have to give up *substitutes* for fulfillment, perhaps the house, the comfortable ways, or familiar friends that made him or her happy in the past."

There seems to be little that men and women can do to reduce the conflicts that arise in breaking free of society's value system. But conflicts with parents, spouses, employers and others are not the result of someone's leaving a symbol-burdened society. These conflicts are the result of the fear we have of facing ourselves. Friends feel as if their beliefs are being questioned. Coworkers, who may not be prepared to consider getting out, resent someone doing what they dare not even think of. "Nothing," says Charles Reich, "makes us angrier than the fear that some pleasure is being enjoyed by others, which is forever denied to us." "Expect nothing from society," says psychiatrist Viscott, "It will do what it can to undermine you. There will always be 'rednecks' waiting to see you fall flat on your face."

If you're aware of the potential conflicts, willing to take the risks and want to change your life, where do you begin?

It became apparent during my interviews with men and women who had changed their lives that they began, not by changing their jobs, nor by moving to another city nor by giving up the material things they had acquired. They began by changing themselves.

What they told me was that they began, often with the help of a therapist, by learning who they were. Once they'd begun to know themselves the rest came easy. If in time they did change jobs or move to another city or give up certain symbols of a previous life it was with a sense of casting off one more link of a chain that could no longer bind them to the past.

We asked each of these men and women what small gift they might like to pass along to others who were trapped in a life that was not of their own making. These are some of the thoughts they wanted to present:

Admit to yourself how you feel about your life now.

Stop giving other people veto power over your life.

Try to feel the difference between the "good" reason you do things and the *real* reason you do them.

Make your choices on the basis of movement toward growth, not out of fear.

Find out where you're getting your approval from, inside or outside?

Stop blaming others for what you do.

Stop blaming others for what you don't do.

If you don't *enjoy* your job, start making plans to *change* it.

Risk being open.

Replace outside goals with your own.

Stop living a prescribed way of life.

Forget about what "they" might think and "they" might say.

Start looking at people's faces on the street. Does it make you uncomfortable? Find out why.

Plan some time to be alone each day and do it.

Instead of zeroing in on a particular life-style, think about change.

Reject goals which have been set for you by others.

You can't reach your center by applying outside values.

Develop your own style and pattern of life.

Learn to love yourself before you expect others to love you.

A million times a day, ask yourself, "How am I feeling right now?"

Want what *you* want, not what you think you *should* want.

Practice doing nothing. How you feel doing nothing will tell you something.

Confront your hatred before it turns to self-pity.

Be open to change. How can you grow if you don't change?

The less self-awareness you have, the less you are free.

Stop being afraid of disapproval.

Admit you're lonely.

You can do anything you want.

Don't expect someone to love you just because you love them.

What is holding you back from your dreams?

Whom do you have to get permission from?

Say "no" to the need to be taken care of.

Stop trying to conform.

You can only love in proportion to your independence.

What do you want?

Always retain your right to say "no."

Nobody can teach you anything, you have to *learn* it.

You have more than one kind of ability.

Everywhere you are is the best possible place to be.

Do what you would if you didn't have to earn a living.

Is this really what you want?

Why? Why not?

How will your excuses for not having lived look to you when you're on your deathbed?

Who says you have to live the rest of your life the way you're living it now?

Stop delivering yourself up to *things*.

Stop trying to live up to the Joneses, start living up to you.

All your important battles are fought within yourself.

Are you living in a world of duty, obligation, role, and loyalty?

Nothing stays the same.

What are you afraid of?

You are responsible for everything you do.

You have run out of scapegoats.

There are no hidden meanings.

Are you hunting for the meat or for the trophies?

Nobody will ever understand you.

You can only have what you are willing to give up.

Nature is a source, not just an escape.

Stop waiting for tomorrow.

You can't be completely independent of the system.

Start dealing with the way things *are*, instead of the way they *ought* to be.

Do not play a role that requires you to be different from what you really are.

You can best contribute to your fellow man by affirming yourself.

Like the most progressive corporations, diversify.

You can't be a success until you do what fulfills you.

Love isn't everything, but it helps.

Learn to see through your illusions.

Start putting *your* needs first.

Having a job is not the purpose of life.

What does fate have to do with it?

What happens if your dream comes true?

The rewards far outweigh the risks.

How about playing the rest of your life by ear?

Is this what you want to be doing ten years from now?

Stop trying to substitute one zero for another.

You can't possibly ever know for sure.

Stop trying to lie to yourself.

Whose voice are you listening to?

You are the only person who controls your life.

Why wait until you retire—you might not make it.

What have you done for you today?

If what psychiatrist David Viscott says is true, that "from society you can expect nothing," where is one to turn for help in growing toward the potential human being he can become?

Can we not turn to friends and parents, our minister,

or friendly neighborhood psychiatrist? Perhaps, but Viscott and others warn against talking things over with "someone who is incapable of offering anything but negative responses because of his own point of view. . . . Remember that people are not used to seeing someone become free and fulfill himself. It frightens them and the only way they can deal with you is to categorize you as having gone off the deep end."

Of the more than fifty-eight couples interviewed in researching this book, nearly forty-two said they first began to get in touch with their own values through human-potential programs of one kind or another. If there is one institution that appears to offer a shred of encouragement to men and women looking for a way out of the rat race, the human-potential movement seems to be it.

The group encounters and sensitivity training "labs" offered by more than one hundred and fifty "growth centers" around the United States are no overnight development. The NTL Institute for Applied Behavioral Science and other management training organizations have been offering sensitivity training since the mid-fifties. But these programs have been pretty much restricted to corporate presidents and other executives for whom increased sensitivity was seen as a road to better management.

Follow-up studies conducted by NTL and others indicate that self-awareness seems to bring about similar results, whether it's gained in a management setting or a free-spirited growth center. Within twelve months after attending company-sponsored sensitivity training programs, about 10 percent of the executive participants leave the corporate world to build lives of their own on farms, operate their own small craft shops, boat yards, motels, and small resorts, or teach or go back to school for graduate degrees that will enable them to do something they may have once dreamed of doing.

Programs conducted by many growth centers around the United States seem made to order for men and women who want to change more than just their careers:

Quest
3000 Connecticut Ave. NW
Washington, D.C. 20008
(301–652–0697)
Letting Go: Often we become frozen in the middle of our emotions and are possessed by a monotony of feelings from which there seems to be no escape. Like the persons of *Brave New World*, we sacrifice high joy rather than risk rejection, love rather than risk anger. We don't move off-center. In this workshop, an atmosphere of openness and trust, games, movement and encounter, will encourage participants to experience a fuller range of their feelings, whatever they might be, thereby expanding their potential for experiencing their own vital limits.

Oasis
20 East Harrison St.
Chicago, Ill. 60605
(312–927–5964)
Be Free: We will work toward discovering the joy of caring and being cared for. Learn to handle the "pulling in" impulse that stops you at new thresholds. A place to find closeness and connectedness,

to get rid of your natural tendency to defend and inhibit yourself, or literally shrink yourself. We will work on learning how to take risks willingly, toward finding the courage and freedom to face and act upon our natural aliveness. Here, you can learn to experience and to listen, to give and to receive, to find, in aloneness, the joy that appears whenever body, mind, and spirit are one. Creative movement, fantasy, Gestalt, and play methods will be used.

Anthos
24 East 22nd Street
New York, New York
(212-673-9067)
Weekend Workshop in Self-Awareness: This workshop is based on the realization that our personal growth is often blocked because we do not see ourselves clearly, see ourselves as others see us, or act as we really feel. The objective of this workshop is to guide participants to become more aware of themselves and others. By creating a supportive atmosphere, participants can experience themselves at a deeper level than daily life provides. Techniques such as psychodrama, encounter and body awareness will be used.

Esalen Institute
1776 Union St.
San Francisco, Calif. 94123
(415-771-1710)
Refocusing Energy: Since many persons spend time dwelling on negative aspects of their personalities and lives, this weekend will be an opportunity to refocus attention on forgotten positive strengths

and individually available tools for continued personal growth and expansion of life possibilities. Approaches from encounter, Gestalt and psychosynthesis will be used.

Flint-Cohen Encounters
6319 Tone Court
Bethesda, Maryland 20034
(301-229-2182)
Loving Triangle: The loving triangle represents a here and now approach to learning. Using a variety of techniques—Gestalt, sensory aliveness, bioenergetics and creative ritual, we try to reach moments of involvement, clarity and insight, and joy for ourselves and group members. As consultants, we try to be ideal group members, and as such, stay actively involved as we struggle to disclose ourselves to each other and the group. Since we see ourselves not as leaders, but as facilitators, we are free to play a variety of roles in helping participants work through entanglements with each other and historical others. We try to create an open culture filled with potential learning situations.

George and Mary Calminson, both in their mid-thirties and parents of a nine-year-old son, are one couple who found their way to a new life and a better understanding of themselves through group encounters.

George Calminson was making out all right with the printing company he worked for in San Francisco, even if he hadn't arrived at the executive suite. But he was on the verge of a promotion to superintendent of a large printing plant, one of several owned by the company that employed him. The job was a goal he'd worked for, and promised a big increase in income. It was but the thickness of a wall away from the prestige of a paneled office and a corporate title, perhaps vice-president.

He'd invested a lot of himself in being in control and even when he was home sick, phone calls from the plant could be answered from the file of specifications, delivery dates, paper stocks and typefaces and press schedules he carried around in his head.

But George Calminson was carrying around something besides printing specifications. "I was trying to live up to an image of supercompetency. I was supergood in the eyes of the company, but I was setting up conditions that were keeping me tight and draining all my energy. I was making myself sick. I was having migraine headaches and asthma attacks.

"I didn't have enough energy left at the end of the day for any kind of relationship with my wife. The job drained me and work became an excuse for not getting into sex. I'd never even thought about such things as the fullness of life. I always thought in terms of having a secure financial base and a secure image defined by my work."

For Mary Calminson, life was "one-dimensional" and she felt locked into being a mother to her son, her sick husband, and the world in general. "I thought it was important for me to be in control and be wise and patient, and be a friend to everybody." But during the past few years of her marriage, Mary Calminson was slowly become more aware that she wanted to be different. She knew that something would have to give.

One morning George couldn't make himself go to work. He "was sitting at the kitchen table having a mi-

graine and looking terrible," when Mary asked him what
he'd really like to do, "right now." George told her he'd
like to "go camping alone."

George headed for the desert but made a detour to Big
Sur and Esalen. "I knew about it, but I really didn't know
what was done there. I'd heard it was sexy and violent,
all those taboo things." George signed up for the first
thing he could, an encounter week, and decided to leave
his future to fate. He didn't really believe "fate" was the
answer but he didn't know what else to do then.

Although the notion he gained at Esalen that he was
responsible for his own life, was completely new to him,
he felt "that it was instantly, obviously right." He experienced a lot more physical involvement with people
than he'd ever had in his adult life; "that was frightening," he said, "and it was also satisfying."

For the first time as an adult, he was able to cry. "I'd
had so little of that kind of release before, but as soon
as I was able to talk about the things I'd been keeping
from myself I experienced some of the sorrow and
loneliness I'd never let myself feel before." Now, George
Calminson says, he's crying three or four times a year,
"which compared to my previous life is like crying every
other day."

When George got home from Esalen, Mary says she
could "*feel* the difference in him." When he came
through the door tears were running down his face and
"he was such a different, beautiful person," that Mary
decided to take the next month's rent money "to go and
get some of whatever it was that George got" at Esalen.

"It was a hard decision for me," she says, "even
though the idea sounded terrific. I had a lot of fears built
up. I was terrified that I'd go down there and be lost in
an ocean of sexuality that would swarm over me."

When her week at Esalen was over most members of her group were surprised to learn she was married and had a child. "I'd worked on so much of my own stuff down there, old hang-ups I'd brought into my relationship with George that I didn't talk very much about our marriage."

For George and Mary Calminson it didn't all come out at once, "But what we did get out of it were some tools for talking with each other and for releasing our emotions. During our weeks at Esalen, we each got a glimmer of another way of being that might be possible for us."

Mary feels that a lot of couples are afraid of the kind of self-discovery and renewal she and George experienced. "I think they fear rocking the boat and changing things between them. They may not feel they're ideally happy, but at least the glue seems to be holding pretty well. But the glue doesn't give any flexibility to grow."

Now George and Mary feel they're *living* together in the space they used to share "as roommates." George doesn't have headaches. It's been a long time since he had an asthma attack. He didn't accept the promotion that was offered him. He quit the rat race instead.

Do you have to be a special kind of person to get out of the rat race? Michael Murphy, cofounder of Esalen Institute, should know. "I think," he says, "it takes personal security of a certain kind. It requires the ability to take risks and it takes a sort of trust in life; that you're going to land right-side-up."

How many people have been to Esalen? "Well, since 1962 I'd say about 50,000 at Big Sur, plus several thousand more at San Francisco. Warren Bennis (President of the University of Cincinnati and fellow of the NTL Institute for Applied Behavioral Science) estimates that

six or seven million people have been in one kind of
encounter group or another. That may seem a little high,
but Bennis is a pretty conservative guy."

Murphy concludes that "it's crucial that a lot of people
make life changes. People are getting oriented into certain niches in society as if they're going to last forever;
sort of like the bus driver who thinks there will always be
busses. Well, there aren't always going to be busses.
Things are changing."

In the final analysis, breaking free of "outside"-
imposed values and goals seems not to be a problem of
finances, or mechanics, or logistics, or of changing jobs.
Breaking free is being able to find your *own* answer when
you get around to asking yourself what it is you want out
of life.

10

Where Will the Money Come From?

What is the largest single inhibiting factor that holds men and women to jobs they want desperately to leave behind them? One simple question: Where will the money come from? How can I meet mortgage payments, pay the doctor bills, feed and clothe my children? What if I get hurt, or sick, and can't work? What about my group health insurance policy? My company-sponsored life insurance premiums, my retirement benefits? Will I have to take my kids out of private schools? How can I maintain two cars, keep up my membership in the Union Club, or the country club? Does this mean I'll have to stop buying my clothes at Brooks Brothers?

These are serious questions, some obviously more pressing than others, and there is no simple or reliably comforting answer to any of them. Those who have broken out, however, seem to agree on at least one essential premise—the shift from corporate life to independence isn't *necessarily* a shift from prosperity to grinding need, but it helps enormously to have accepted at the outset the very real possibility of crucial changes in lifestyle.

The things that money can buy, after all, can only be bought with money. And the first truth about breaking out is that there is likely to be less money than there was before.

On the other hand, the impetus to break out arises from the need to have more of the things money *can't* buy, and the trade-off has to be a serious one if the adjustment is to work.

Many corporate escapees, for example, complain about company pressure to conform to a specific pattern of social life and consumer consumption. They were, they felt, expected to live in a home that seemed roughly compatible with their corporate salary range; drive a car (or cars) that met the same loosely defined standard; eat in restaurants where they were not destined, unavoidably, to be seated next to their boss (but also where they were not likely to rub elbows with the mail clerks or members of the steno pool). Once free of those pressures, one is also free of the compulsion to live in high-cost urban areas, where the real estate market fluctuations rarely have anything to do with the intrinsic worth of housing, and everything to do with the intangibles of snob zoning, proximity to industrial or other corporate entities (universities, for example), and the agility of municipal fund raisers.

In short, the answer to the mortgage problem is to sell the house, unload the mortgage, and go somewhere where you can put a roof over your head without wrecking the family budget.

Wally Dinsmore, for example, was an engineer in California, earning $26,000 a year. "In Sacramento," he says, "we had a lovely home with a parklike yard, a new station wagon and a late-model camper pick-up." But at forty-one, Dinsmore quit his job with Aerojet General, and bought a farm a few miles from the one-store town of Umpquoa, Oregon. The land had not been farmed for several years, and the Dinsmores found a rundown two-story house with an 1891-vintage kitchen, a wood cook stove and a sagging floor. There was no bathroom or indoor plumbing, and the electrical wiring was faulty. "Four months after moving in," recalls Dinsmore, "we got hot running water. We celebrated by taking a shower —and ran the well dry." Several emergencies and a few months later, Dinsmore is building a herd of cattle and a flock of sheep, grows his feed on his own land, and includes chickens, a horse, two dogs and a cat among the family menagerie. His three children (Laurie, twelve, Bill, ten, and Susan, seven) "have matured. They have responsibilities now, yet they also have more freedom. This place is so beautiful and peaceful, I wonder why we waited so long."

Mike Mitchell, a $35,000-a-year Wall Street insurance broker, is now running an inn on Christmas Cove, an island 60 miles north of Portland, Maine, and used to live in a comfortable home in a wooded part of Rowayton, Conn. He commuted to New York a "convivial hour each way by train and another twenty minutes by subway." "He was," said a *Life* magazine reporter, "drinking and smoking and getting fat." Mike Mitchell and his wife heard about an inn for sale in January, 1969, and drove up to Maine to look it over. The property they discovered, and shortly bought for about $90,000 ($15,000 down), included a 12-bedroom Victorian inn, a 10-unit lodge, a restaurant that seated more than 100, a gift shop, a grocery store and assorted guest houses and docks spread out over 23 acres. The Mitchells housed some 350 guests that first summer, a near-capacity crowd, but the costs of renovation were high, and they lost about $2,000 for the season. Christmas Cove Inn is now running smoothly, with no more than the predictable upkeep, but Mike Mitchell figures he'll be lucky to clear as much as $10,000 for the 1973 season. Even so, says Mitchell, he wonders why it took him so long to make the break.

Jack McClintock and his wife gave up an income of $20,000 a year, two cars, and a house on the Gulf of Mexcio, "exactly the life we had been working toward for over five years." However, decided the McClintocks, "it wasn't as much fun as we thought it should be; we were missing out on life." So they sold everything but their books, records, and pictures, loaded them into a VW bus and took off to see America. The McClintocks live "nicely" on $300 a month, and when money gets tight (Jack McClintock is a free-lance writer), his wife, a social worker with four years of college, works as a waitress for a week or two, while Jack picks beans or takes on other odd jobs.

Jack Fuller, on the other hand, refused to burn his bridges behind him. A graduation accessories salesman from Akron, Ohio (earning more than $30,000 a year in 1962), Jack Fuller and his wife Lee rented their colonial house, stored their furniture, and moved with their two young daughters to a federal housing project in an Alaskan whaling village named Point Hope, where both were given teaching jobs by the Bureau of Indian Affairs. The Fullers had no telephone and no plumbing; in the winter they melted ice for water, and in the summer they hauled it from a well. Tracked down eight years later by a reporter from *Life* magazine, Fuller was living "comfortably" in Nome, Alaska, where he earned $14,000 a year as a full-time director of the National Guard Eskimo Scouts. Lee earns an additional $6,000 working part time for the National Park Service. The Fullers have long since sold their home in Akron, and have no thought of returning.

The pattern, clearly, is varied. Some corporation dropouts have gotten out of the home mortgage business altogether, living in trailers, or tents, or schooners, in microbuses, or rented rooms. Some have built their own homes, discovering skills they never thought they had, or enlisting the aid of skilled craftsmen willing to work side by side with them. And others have simply shifted their base of operations, moving from the inflated real estate markets of the major urban areas to areas where perfectly serviceable homes, farms, inns and other land is available for a fraction of what they had been paying in Croton-on-Hudson, or Darien, or Cambridge, or Menlo Park.

However, a corporate dropout still unsure of his move can usually follow the Jack Fuller tactic. Put your furniture in storage, and rent your house for as much as you need to cover the mortgage, taxes, and normal upkeep. It may even pay you, as it did the Youlands, to take out a second mortgage on the property, in order to help finance the scheme you've settled on as a means of making your way back into the world.

The most important point, however, is the most obvious one. Whatever its charm, location, comforts, or symbolic presence, your house is a *material thing,* and it can't help you sleep better at night, reduce the burdens of corporate life, or be a substitute for the satisfaction you'll get out of taking control, at last, of your life. Your house, as bankers are fond of reminding you, is likely to be the most costly single investment you make during the course of your life. If your mortgage is what is keeping you from making a break from a life that's eating you up, bit by bit, get rid of the house, before it gets rid of you.

Medical bills are another problem. Even happy people break legs, get water on the knee, and have children susceptible to chicken pox. And there is no avoiding the fact that prepaid group medical insurance is probably the most economical way of assuring your family that it will get the medical care it needs, particularly in case of emergencies. Blue Cross, however, isn't going to show you out the back door just because you've given up your spot in the executive parking lot, turned in your plastic plant, and taken to spending your evenings with your children. In some communities, individuals or their families may join "community health plans," a sort of collective medical practice which provides the same services, often at reduced costs, as most prepaid group health insurance policies. The Harvard Community Health Plan, for example, services some 32,000 families in Metropolitan Boston, providing them with complete preventative, diagnostic, emergency and general medical care for annual package prices that average out to $804 per family. The package includes hospitalization, some psychiatric and dental care, most obstetrical and gynecological costs, and continuing outpatient care in medical clinics designed to help participants in this medical care program ward off serious illness *before* it develops and while, where possible, its effects can still be controlled.

Whatever the case, anyone contemplating a break from the corporate shelter should look carefully at the list of medical benefits he's been paying for.

"If you have a laundry list of medical things that need doing," say scores of former organization men, "have them taken care of while you're still on the corporation's group insurance plan. If the kids don't have their tonsils out, see about having them taken care of if they've been giving them trouble. If your back's been bothering you, have it looked at, you can at least establish that it got that way while you were on the payroll. If you've been thinking about a vasectomy, maybe now is the time to do it. Unexpected children have a way of changing your plans. Some corporate health insurance programs cover certain dental costs. See if yours is one that does."

Ted Jackson, father of four and former auto company regional sales manager, had his doctor go over every member of the family looking for anything that might be wrong or that could go wrong. During his last year with the company Ted's wife had an ear operation to restore partial loss of hearing, two kids had tonsils and adenoids out, his high-school-age son had a knee operation, and Ted had a vasectomy and hernia repair. Jackson saved $8,000 he might have had to pay out of reduced income later on.

Saving money on food and clothing is really nothing more than doing all the things we've known about all along but lacked either the will or the inclination to fol-

low through on. We've always known that Sears, Roebuck clothes are likely to be less expensive than the wor-
sted woolens at Brooks Brothers, but many clothes
horses may not be aware that they're paying for labels,
a modicum of deference, and the opportunity to avoid
crowds. In any case, making ends meet on clothes tends
to be among the least complicated problems faced by
corporate refugees.

One of the first things they realize is that the function
of a shirt is to cover the chest and arms, more or less, to
keep out rain, cold, dust, bright sunlight, and to comfort
the sensibilities of those tender souls unnerved by the
sight of a naked shoulder. Shirts are *not,* on the other
hand, proof of sexual competence, badges of social dis-
tinction, proof of alertness to fashion modes, or the crucial difference between success and failure in American
business or academic or professional life. The same ar-
gument, roughly applied, goes for pants, socks, shoes,
and even neckties. This is not to deny the aesthetic impulse, but rather to ask that it be confronted squarely.
Wear a shirt that *you* like, and think about why you like
it. The chances are you'll find one just like that at Sears,
or Morgan Memorial, or Goodwill, or even in your
grandfather's sea chest.

And when you find one you like, *wear it.* Don't throw
it away because you wear a hole in the elbow, or fray the
collar, or rip a seam, or lose a button. Rediscover the
needle and thread (even men, curiously, have learned
the intricacies of threading needles, and then pushing
the needle into and out of an interesting range of cloth
fabrics, in a "previously determined" manner). Most
people spend something like ten times what they need to
on clothes, largely because they are too impatient, or
lazy, to see to perfectly conventional repairs; and partly

because they make the mistake of imagining that they can achieve, through their wardrobes, what they haven't been able to demonstrate by sheer force of character or will. Don't believe that clothes make the man. And if you find yourself tempted to do so, keep firmly before you an image of the last anxiety-ridden, self-doubting, ulcer-tortured corporate automaton you saw walking around in a $300 suit.

A final word on buying clothes: keep in mind that most large clothing or shoe manufacturers have retail outlets for what they call "seconds," items that fail, for one reason or another, to meet assembly-line inspection standards. These items are sold at sharply reduced prices, and their defects may be simple matters such as ragged stitching, faulty zippers, dye stains, or whatever. Only rarely are the defects alarming enough to warrant unusual caution, and for large families, these "seconds" outlets can represent very comfortable savings.

Cutting back on the food budget is another common-sense problem with fairly evident solutions. As a rule of thumb, almost everything you do in the kitchen—as opposed to paying someone else to do it for you, at the governing minimum wage for farm, food processing, and grocery wholesale and retail workers—will save you money. In the long run, you can make bread more cheaply than you can buy it; you can put sugar on your cornflakes at a fraction of the cost of "sugar-frosted flakes"; you can make enough vanilla pudding to feed a family of six for what you pay for a half-ounce can of pudding prepared in a factory hundreds of miles away; and so on. Every housewife (and most husbands) know this obvious truth, but the precooked food and packaging industries continue to flourish all the same.

If you're going to give up that hefty executive salary in

order, among other things, to spend more time with your family and with your hands, then spend some part of that togetherness in the kitchen. Cook your *own* steak, bake your own potatoes, toss your own green salad; even splurge a little, with a good vineyard-bottled $3 Bordeaux. You and your wife will have more time together, and a better meal, for only a little more than it would cost you to hire a babysitter, and park the car—*before* you even set foot in the "Bubbles and Beef," or wherever it is you normally go when you wish to share in that familiar and invariably fruitless American expedition in search of a decent restaurant meal.

A great many corporate dropouts have taken the logical step, *vis-à-vis* their food problem, of cutting through the tangle of growers, gatherers, shippers and grocers. Thirty-seven-year-old Brown Bergen, for example, served his industry tour of duty as an insurance man, and then as a computer systems analyst. After making his break at the age of twenty-eight, Bergen studied photography until his savings ran out, taught English at a small school in Massachusetts, and finally took a mortgage out on sixteen acres of land in Hillsdale, New York, where he and his wife Jeanne cleared and cultivated a garden that now provides them three meals a day.

"With a carpenter friend," notes a reporter from the *Wall Street Journal,* "Brown more than doubled the size of the tiny house on the land. Meantime, he and Jeanne took up skiing, became expert at it, and took part-time jobs as skiing instructors. Brown also went to work teaching again, for a local high school. But what he found there was a 'junior league' version of the system he'd escaped, so, in 1969, he signed up with a carpenter and spent six months learning the trade. Now he skis, carpenters, gardens and photographs. He and Jeanne obtain nearly all their own food from an organic garden they cultivate themselves, using no pesticides or chemical fertilizers. For the first time in his life, Bergen says, he has lost his unwillingness to get up in the morning."

All these families, the Mitchells, the Bergens, the Fullers, and others, share, at the least, an attitude toward their decision to break away from a relatively secure—if oppressive—economic situation, in favor of a great deal of chance-taking. Their "security," they believed, was more transparent than real, and the trade-off—between the assurance of regular income and the gathering costs of obeisance to the system—was simply not workable or reassuring. As a consequence, few of these families felt that they were *sacrificing* anything in order to make time for wanderlust. Instead, they believed they were *gaining* something a great deal more valuable; each divestment of a material possession became an act of liberation, a share in their portfolio of self-actualizing truths.

The idea, of course, is a romantic one, and even the mercurial Larry Murphy thought to survey his options before slamming the door on his high-salaried job at Pan American.

Murphy took classes in pottery-making at San Francisco State College to learn the hobby that turned into a full-time occupation. He equipped his basement shop while still employed, and produced commercial quantities during his days at home to make sure he had everything he needed, and to see how much time would be required to turn out enough pottery to make a living.

Larry and his wife Rose traveled to art shows and street markets to sell his mugs and plates and cups *before* he quit his job, to learn how well his pottery could be expected to sell. Larry talked with potters and other craftsmen to get a feel for the income he could expect to earn.

When he and Rose determined that he could expect to make about $12,000 a year, they started living on *that* income, to see how it would feel, even though he continued to bring home his considerably higher pilot's pay.

If your new way of life calls for buying a farm or a small business, or a truck or boat or some other vehicle, do it before you leave the corporate umbrella. You may find, as other men have, that you lose your credit rating when you turn your back on the prerogatives of executive life.

Ralph Graham was unable to finance a small home while studying for his Ph.D. even though his payment record had always been excellent. David Youland was turned down by three savings and loan banks before finally borrowing money at a commercial bank to help finance his hunting and fishing camp.

Gerald Higgins used to get unsolicited credit cards when he was an executive for the telephone company. His wife received notes in the mail advising her that charge accounts had been opened in her name at exclusive shops and boutiques in suburban Cleveland where they lived. But when Gerald left the phone company to become an artist, his wife was unable to open an account at J. C. Penney's to save on January white sales and children's clothing.

Some men, artists, writers, craftsmen, and others, have incorporated themselves under solid-sounding company names so they could obtain commercial discounts for supplies and travel expenses and to facilitate credit.

Clearly, there are practical steps to be considered by even the most resolute corporate dropout.

Step one: Accept the probability that the money supply will shrink, and start thinking hard about unloading your accumulation of material *things*. Be prepared to sell your house, cash in your stocks, resign from your clubs, borrow on your life insurance, and get rid of your surplus furniture, recreation equipment, and all the other stuff you once thought you'd never be able to get along without. You need not assume you will *have* to take all these drastic steps, but if you're prepared for them, they'll become a great deal less painful. You may even begin to look forward to the idea.

Step two: Think very hard about what, exactly, you want to do. Now that you have come to terms with the problem of your possessions, you can allow yourself an unrestricted look at the apparent options before you. Now that you've unloaded the house, you can unload the maid, and all the other expenses of upkeep. Your budget is simpler, and quite a bit more modest. So if you want to go to Alaska to teach Eskimos, or to Florida to grow grapefruit, or to your basement to weave tapestries, there is very little to hold you back. But you ought to be sorting these things out *before* you pull up the anchor, at least if you want to work toward a smooth transition. Don't make the mistake of working out a hypothetical budget for your newly liberated life, and then sorting out your options with that budget in mind. That's where you were in the first place, and you've got to wrench yourself away from that sort of cost accounting, at least until you've found the thing *you* want, as opposed to the job you're forced to take in order to meet your projected standard of living.

In the long run, the material difference is likely to be marginal. You'll always find a way to produce the reve-

nue you need. But psychologically, you need that moment of exquisite open-endedness. It is your best and
quickest way to become the majority stockholder in an
enormously profitable enterprise, the new you.

If you don't know, frankly, what you want to do with
yourself, and need time to consider the possibilities, *take*
the time. Consider not working at all for a few weeks, or
even a few months. Depending on what you had in the
bank to begin with, and what you are likely to have once
you've unloaded your hoard of chrome, engine parts,
brick, mortar, Naugahyde, and golf clubs, consider taking your family on a leisurely trip, across the country, to
Canada, or wherever it is you've been planning to go
once you had a little vacation time saved up, and you
could duck an annual sales meeting or put aside the
annual report you'd promised by Monday morning. Buy
or rent a camper bus, and hit the road. Or if you know
your way around mainsails and jibs, buy yourself a
schooner and set sail. Somewhere along the way, the
right idea will simply be there, and you'll know instantly
where you're going next, and why.

Step three: (For those who want it all settled before the
big break.) *Plan ahead.* Once you've decided on the other
life you really want to lead, give it an extramural try. If
it is possible to "do" the thing on weekends, or on vacations, see if your skills measure up, or find out how
difficult it will be to develop them to the point that they
are likely to provide the income you think you'll need. If
it's a matter of moving to a new area, say Florida or
Maine, look it over during the off-season months. Consider Florida in August, and Maine in early February. Be
sure you're planning your new life around a twelve-
month calendar year. Look over the real estate values,

the quality of the public (or private) schools. Look into the state and municipal tax situation before you pick a permanent location. Find yourself a local banker, and ask his candid advice about home financing, the likelihood of small loans for new businesses. Talk it over with your family; if the decision isn't jointly arrived at, it may not be jointly applauded, and its consequences may not be jointly endured.

Step four: (For those who can't seem to figure out an alternative, but know they've got to break out.) *Don't plan ahead.* Waiting for ideal circumstances is about like waiting "until you can afford a baby," or vowing to "go back to school and finish up later on." Which is to say, it hardly ever happens. If this is your hang-up, bite the bullet. Go back to step two, make your break, give yourself some time to sort it all out, and have confidence that something sensible will occur. Most importantly, grasp the fact that you need a change; uncertainty about the future is less debilitating, all things considered, than the certainties about your present situation, and the direction it seems to be taking with your life.

One final note: Though "breaking out" is apparently a high-risk decision, and its chances of success, in the psychological sense, may depend upon your willingness to do without a great many of the artifacts of conventional corporate achievement, it does not follow that corporate dropouts have been reduced to the status of public wards, or that their children go barefoot in the wintertime.

As a practical matter, a great many dropouts live better than they ever did before, and not only in the sense that they are more at peace with themselves and with their families. The qualities that earned most of these men their high salaries in the old life, coupled with their new resolve and an infinitely better frame of mind, invariably contribute to their *new* lives, and to their income potential, governed by its new framework of assumptions.

In the 1970s, the average corporate dropout seems to be earning somewhere between $10,000 and $15,000 per year, and thriving on it. There are fewer expense-account lunches, fewer three-button suits, and fewer two-car garages, but also sharply reduced housing costs, new assumptions about the needed range of material possessions, and a great many new skills—of the sort that plumbers and electricians provide for $12 per hour, and up.

Leaving the corporate way of life doesn't mean giving up money, or even any of the things money can buy. What it probably *does* mean is a set of attitudes about what is worth having, and how much of yourself can or ought to be compromised in pursuit of it. So don't agonize about "where the money will come from." That isn't the problem now, and it never was.

11

What Can the Corporations Do?

What can corporations do to reduce the number of defections among the brightest and most impressive of their middle management executives? Probably the single most effective thing corporations can do, industrial psychologists seem to agree, is to place decision-making power in the hands of the men in immediate contact with the facts.

As Psychological Assessment Associates' Marshall Heyman puts it, "The way things are in many corporations today, the more important a decision, the greater the likelihood that it will be made by people who are ignorant—removed from the data and the real problem. The more a problem gets kicked upstairs, the more it's taken away from reality; the tremendous complexity of the problem has to be more and more reduced so that it winds up on not more than one page, preferably with a central operative paragraph.

"If large corporations are going to continue to exist in

America, and if they are going to hang on to really good innovative men, which they must do to maintain their size, I would recommend decentralization, putting the men who know back in charge of various operations and letting them run them.

"A lot of people moving up in the corporate structure today realize that someone else makes the decisions they should be making—yet they pay the penalties when things go wrong. These men are tired of that frustration, the wear and tear. They've seen that they can take themselves out of the rat race and do something else."

J. D. Ritchie, British-born president of Asiatic Petroleum Corporation, agrees with P.A.A.'s Dr. Heyman: "We had a discussion in one of the parts of our organization three years ago about a change in working methods that really was going to do away with the old, totally hierarchical, 'everything has to be approved by the boss' type organization, in favor of the sort of organization where far more people were going to have to make decisions and stand behind what they were doing.

"After one of the meetings where this had been discussed with all the people concerned—in fact a lot of the ideas came from them—one of the chaps looked around to a friend of his and said, 'If we go this way, where's my protection?' Well, sometimes making your own decisions isn't comfortable, but for a good man it's a lot more fun.

"I think that Asiatic now is gradually getting things to where most of the decisions are being made by the man who's closest to the situation. But I don't think we've got to the point where people are sure that if they take the right decision and the outcome is wrong, that they won't be blamed for it.

"It's no good our saying, 'We encourage risk-taking,' if we don't give rewards to the risk-takers. That's the most difficult thing to get into any corporate philosophy and practice, I think. It's something we are trying quite deliberately to do in this company. We get decisions quicker that way, and we keep some good people who might otherwise get bored with it all."

What do the experts see in the future of executives with big corporations that get bigger? Dr. Frederick Rockett of the Psychological Corporation is one expert who sees a less than bright picture: "With consolidation of many companies we're going to have larger, more complicated organizations. That, combined with the impact of new government regulations, will reduce the range of entreprenurial opportunity so that we'll get a sort of 'institutionalized' executive.

"With bigger corporations there will be more combat fatigue among executives. I believe we already have a kind of low-grade combat fatigue among executives generally. The result is a reduced inclination to take risks, and a greater tendency to avoid decision making."

Some companies' "job enrichment" programs for rank and file employees, restructuring jobs to replace routine and rote with meaningful responsibility, have paid off in improved management morale and reduced executive turnover.

William Van Vorts, clerical supervisor at Merrill, Lynch, Pierce, Fenner and Smith, says: "A year ago I sometimes spent four hours a day on the telephone answering questions from brokers. The processing of stock certificates in my office was so minutely broken down that I was the only one who could handle a question about the end result.

"Today each clerk handles all the work on a certificate and takes responsibility for it. When she rejects an improperly prepared certificate she prepares a report and signs her name and telephone extension to the paper work and handles any calls from the brokers. This cut 70 percent of my phone calls. Now, for the first time, I really have time for planning."

"At the Travelers Insurance Corp., accounting supervisors formerly spent 35 percent of their time answering questions from subordinates and 45 percent doing production work—helping clerks over snags," reports vice-president Russell Sweet. "Now that clerks have more authority and encouragement to solve problems on their own, supervisors can play a more active role in management. The most dramatic effect of our job-enrichment program for clerks has been the way it has improved morale among our supervisory and management people."

As office workers take on tasks the boss used to handle, the boss's job gets more interesting, but Roy Walters, Glen Rock, New Jersey, management consultant isn't content to let job enrichment stop at that. "We're now looking at $20,000- and $25,000-a-year jobs. A year ago the top would be $12,000 to $14,000. Just because a guy has the title of vice president doesn't mean he has an interesting job or that his abilities are being fully used."

"The era of big corporate boards that meet almost every day to make important decisions is just about over, adds Chicago consultant Foster Summer, "when it comes to corporate talent it's a case of 'use it or lose it' and the companies that lose it won't be around very long."

Beyond returning executives to the mainstream of

company decision making, consultants say turnover can be reduced by recognition that every manager's personal values and life goals may not be the same.

Bernard Haldane, long-time management consultant and recruiter says, "industry tends to discourage people from being open about, for example, not wanting to become president. Everybody is pushed in that direction. His wife, children, boss and his associates push him. People get destroyed that way.

"I know a man who worked with financial matters. He handled figures and systems for a manufacturing company that applied his work in the areas of distribution and sales. He'd found ways of cutting distribution costs and worked out a new method of sales compensation that proved more equitable. He was promoted to assistant vice president and then vice president in charge of merchandising. After two years he'd practically wrecked the company because merchandising wasn't what really turned him on. What turned him on was figures; not people.

"He was a victim of the system that says, 'You've got to keep getting higher and higher management jobs, that's what development means.'

"One of the problems of—and with—top management is that employees don't believe getting ahead in the company must be their goal in life, but the employers *do* believe it. In general, the output of people, executives included, has dropped and dropped. Most psychologists I know feel that very few people produce as high as 20 percent of their potential, which means that four times as much can be done as is being done now."

Says Marshall Heyman: "Our society has a mystique about advancement; that as a man moves up in his company he's more successful because he's invested with more responsibility and more authority and so on and everybody stands up and applauds him. But his job swallows more and more of his energies and leaves less and less crawl space for his personal life. Beyond that, he has less and less freedom in terms of what he, as a manager, is able to do.

"Take the man who is offered a promotion and says he'd rather stay where he is. I have yet to see a corporation that values such a response. I can't think of a single organization.

"The choice the engineer, or the salesman or the accountant, is forced to make today is between the things that give him intrinsic satisfaction and the things that make for social values and corporate advancement. If he's going to go the social values route he has to give up his engineering or sales or whatever it is he loves doing; a little bit to begin with, a hell of a lot along the way.

"I remember being in a screening interview with a guy who was just completing his engineering education, and he said that if you want a future in our society you can't count on being an engineer more than ten years, because if you're a successful engineer you'll be identified as a comer and you'll start getting into the executive suite where you'll be doing less and less engineering.

"I have always valued the idea that organizations could be structured to honor and reward the good people who want to continue to be good at whatever it is they love doing. But the problem with achieving that is, it takes a pretty big employer to accept that *his* goals are not necessarily his *employees'* goals, without taking that fact as a rejection of himself."

Asiatic Petroleum Corporation is one employer that

never twists anyone's arm when it comes to taking on more responsibility. "We have just now started a system," says President Ritchie, "of posting all job vacancies below the very top levels. If we think there's somebody who ought to put himself up as a candidate for a particular job, we might say to him, 'Aren't you interested in putting yourself up for this thing?' But if he says, 'No I'm happy where I am,' nobody's going to force him. We respect his life and how he wants to live it.

"I can give you an example of how well I think this is going to work out for us. I meet every month with a dozen people from different parts of the company. I give them coffee and we just talk about the company. It's understood that I'm not trying to gather information that will be the source of action.

"Not long ago we discovered that only two people in the group, including myself, had not, within the last three years, decided to resign. Ten out of twelve, myself included, had actually gone so far as to draft a letter of resignation.

"Of the two people who hadn't, both had been twenty years with the company. One had held the same job since the day he joined. He'd had it for twenty years and he did not want to change. Well, he's *clearly* regarded as a very good employee and nobody's going to try and persuade him to do anything but the job he does superbly. The other man had had eight jobs in twenty years and he wouldn't have had his life any differently. So here you have an example of totally different career experiences, both people utterly happy in their jobs, and we completely happy with them."

As the historic values of money, power and prestige give way to individual values, managers no longer accept the minuses of their jobs as "just the way things are." Consultant Bernard Haldane says that, "As people learn what kinds of things really turn them on; the areas in which they are both effective and self-motivated, they will do a great deal to have those areas expanded, and other, less self-motivated areas, lessened. But many of today's senior managers, men in their fifties and sixties who have been trained to think in terms of power, are uncomfortable and, to some extent, I think, resentful of the new breed of employees who want to give less and less of their lives to the corporation and its goals."

For the vast majority of people who are not highly motivated to acquire power, the price of having it thrust upon them is frustration and not enough time or energy for one's own satisfactions. They are removing themselves from that kind of situation.

One of the most destructive of the corporations' practices is the custom of frequent transfers—often simply to "broaden" an individual for the purpose of increasing his usefulness to the company. Just as it *presumes* every employee wants to "get ahead," on its terms, the corporation *presumes* the employee is willing to accept frequent moves as a way of reaching these presumed goals.

About a third of the corporations responding to a United Van Lines survey reported that they had a policy of relocating personnel on a periodic basis. The trend toward increasingly frequent transfers seems to be centered among managers in the twenty-five-year-old to forty-year-old age bracket. Two-thirds of managers contacted in a recent survey reported moving at least once every three years. Twenty percent said they were transferred once a year.

An executive at Humble Oil & Refining Company said

his employer "had no compunction at all about transfer-
ring a man right in the middle of a school year, with little
or no notice at all, into a job that was clearly a lateral
transfer, that may have been vacant for six months or
more."

The executive, who at the time of our interview was
making plans to leave the company, said "Humble has
always been very good about making sure you don't lose
money on your house, even granting allowances for ex-
traordinary expenses, but that's apparently as far as their
understanding of a move goes."

Bethesda, Maryland, consulting psychologist Alvin M.
Cohen points out that corporate policies which tend to
move people around, like crating up a piece of machinery and shipping it to another plant, depersonalize the
entire work relationship and lead to a sense of insignifi-
cance and powerlessness over one's life. "The symptoms
are sometimes, though not always, invisible around the
office, but the price is paid in men's homes, in bed, and
in the center of their gut."

"More and more executives," adds Washington, D.C.,
psychotherapist Isaac Harris, "are refusing employers'
inducements to accept yet another transfer. It gets to the
point where a man asks himself what the purpose of it all
is. A lot of the people I work with are seeing the money
and power and prestige that companies frequently offer
along with a transfer as being really worthless. They have
to admit to themselves that those things wouldn't even
exist if they were the last person on earth, but that some
of their other satisfactions, like fishing, or painting, or
making music, would be just as real. Those are the satisfactions they're opting for today."

One executive's wife, interviewed by Vance Packard

while he was researching *A Nation of Strangers,* told him at the end of the interview, "I've said more than I meant to, but I wanted you to know there is one soul out here ho would like to resign from the rat race!"

Dr. Myrna M. Weissman, codirector of Yale University's Depression Research Unit has found that moving causes far more stress than is generally believed, and contributes to depression among American women.

"When you ask a bunch of depressed people about events that have occurred in their life recently, moving was about the third most frequent event," adds Dr. Weissman. "Among the most frequent victims of transfer-related depression," researchers say, "are middle-class professionals who now constitute America's new migrant worker, especially in the early years of their careers."

Said one manager recently resigned from a Connecticut insurance firm, "There was always a lot of talk around our company about the traditional American ethic of hard work and free enterprise. I think it's time for some of the 'Great American Tradition' preacherw to remember the great American traditions of family and community and the value of close and trusted friends.

"This country wasn't founded on the principle that material goods are the finer things in life, but a bigger paycheck is just about all the continual round of transfers has to offer most of us."

Beyond *not* making managers' jobs any duller than they have to be, and *not* coercing them to accept added responsibilities they don't want, or treating them and their families like objects to be moved at will, what might corporations do, to hang on to managers with an urge to live a better life?

It used to be that pension plans and stock options did

the job pretty well. In the mid-fifties that was what management fringe benefits were all about. Today, many executives see stock options as "only money" and resent the effect some pension plans have on their work relations.

"Our benefit package is a pretty good one," commented a vice president of a North Carolina furniture manufacturer, "but I don't get a penny of it if I leave the company before I'm fifty-five. And when it gets down to basics in my boss's office, I know I'd better not push too hard for something I know is best for the company—if he disagrees with me. It's there in the back of my mind that he can fire my ass and take away all those company benefits from me any time he wants to. Frankly the company would be better off if we all had portable pension plans."

Portable executive retirement programs require a degree of industry acceptance that will be too long in the coming to benefit most managers working today, but other programs being instituted in the United States and abroad bear looking at.

Early retirement is perhaps the most widely practiced new form of executive fringe compensation. Many corporations see early retirement as a means of moving younger, more aggressive people into the top slots. Retiring IBM Chairman T. Vincent Learson says that, "the interests of IBM will best be served by management teams of upcoming young men and women."

In July of 1972, Westinghouse Electric Corporation Chairman Donald C. Burnham announced a "step-down-at-sixty" policy for the company's seven top officers. Burnham contends that "younger executives will be better prepared to meet the new demands and challenges facing business and industry."

Some corporations, Westinghouse included, are shifting toward what some corporations are calling "phased retirement" or "semiretirement" to ease the demands on senior executives. When Chairman Burnham reaches sixty, he'll become an "officer-director" and devote two-thirds of his time—at two-thirds his regular pay—to company business.

Many executives we talked to, men in the thirty-five to fifty-five age bracket, acknowledged they'd like such a plan for themselves right now. "It's reached the point where I'm now giving up time to do what I want to get something I don't need: higher income."

While a program of part-time corporate managers might not work for many key jobs in a lot of companies, it is working now in enough places and in enough professions for the idea to deserve serious consideration. But so far, most of the part-time professionals are women.

Peter Lewis, president of Cleveland, Ohio's Progressive Insurance Company, is so enthusiastic about the part-time clerks he put on the company's payroll not long ago that he says he's going to begin hiring part-time claims adjusters, underwriters, and "the entire gamut of management positions.

"I'm convinced," Lewis adds, "that we'll be able to structure a work schedule permitting five-hour shifts. Why not use these talented, motivated, and well-educated people?"

The Educational Records Bureau, a New York firm that does testing for private schools, employs a female psychologist as part-time market researcher. Grayson & Associates, an Englewood, New Jersey, marketing concern has a part-time office manager who works 25 hours a week, and the Smithsonian Institution has two part-time female lawyers on its staff.

Scores of other companies including several major corporations who'd just as soon not rock the boat right now by publicizing their programs, are experimenting with part-time salesmen, customer engineers, and service representatives. "Right now," they feel, "we're just not sure our customers are ready to accept being taken care of by part-time employees. But after we've tried it a while we'll ask them how they like our service and if they say they're happy we'll publicize what we're doing."

Other businesses—law firms, publishers, public relations, and advertising agencies—have for years employed men in the would-be "full-time" $25,000 to $50,000 income bracket, at long-term, part-time jobs.

Many small corporations, those doing from three to ten million dollars a year in business, have prospered under part-time management. In nearly every case though, the part-time manager is the owner who's reached fifty or sixty years of age and decided he'd rather have time off than a higher figure at the end of his balance sheet.

Psychologist Albert Ellis feels that part-time work may be the answer for executives and others who must do some of the dull, unpleasant jobs. "I wouldn't mind working on a garbage truck or sweeping the streets," he points out, "so long as I only had to do it one hour a day."

Working a four day week is a long way from putting in Albert Ellis' hypothetical one hour day, but it does give employees a 50 percent increase in usable weekend time. Fifty-six percent of responses to a recent Business Week survey were against changing to a four-day work week. But a healthy minority, 41 percent, favored the shorter period.

Howard R. Gessner, vice president of Gayman Industries, Inc., Buffalo, New York, reported his company's manufacturing employees "have been on a four-day week for a year. They favor it and have not registered any complaints about fatigue (the result of a ten-hour work day) restricting their activities.

"Our employees favor the four-day, ten-hour-day week," says Kenneth White, president of White Electronics. "It gives them a three-day weekend which allows time for travel and family outings. Morale is exceptionally high and employee efficiency seems to have improved, resulting in increased production."

Critics of the four-day week say it "will only lead to a further disintegration of family life" and that "few people know how to use leisure time wisely, and too much can be boring or demoralizing or both." None of these problems however, seem to be the experience of workers or families who work the shorter week.

Anthony M. Pasquale, who is employee benefits consultant at Marsh & McLennan, Incorporated, suggests that corporations might benefit from what he calls a "work-at-home" program for managers. "Informally," he says, "such programs have been carried on by thousands of executives over the years," but Pasquale feels that formalizing such a program "would make an attractive addition to formal compensation policy and could provide more effective performance, personal health improvement, and financial advantages."

Pasquale argues that some tasks can be accomplished *only* in isolation from the corporate environment. Anthony Jay, former British Broadcasting Company executive, lists the benefits of working at home as one of the most important discoveries of his life. "An enormous amount of work can be accomplished in a day, given the absence of the corporate nuisance meetings, telephone calls, correspondence, budget reviews and other external demands." Pasquale adds that Anthony Jay's experience has been shared by many Americans, "who also have been astounded by the results of a day's work at home that might take a week at the office."

"The truly committed," observes Pasquale, "are working at or thinking about their responsibilities far more than the boundaries of nine to five will permit. When distractions of a home office are minimal, there is little question about effective performance. An executive can shave or not shave, scream and curse, work in pajamas or a suit; he is free of the distraction of commuting, delays, or interruptions beyond his control, and lengthy lunches."

A regular work-at-home program could also reduce the executive's exposure to pollution, decrease the strain of commuting, and "could make for a psychologically healthier executive," according to Pasquale.

Savings derived from home office tax deductions, reduced commuting, and luncheon costs and possibly even better health, could add up to a goodly sum for the work-at-home executive.

"Educators," concludes Pasquale, "have discovered that responsible people can learn without a formal academic environment and mandatory attendance, just as one does not need to go to church to live by the golden rule. Where it applies, working at home during the normal business day can be a fruitful practice."

The Basel, Switzerland, headquarters of chemical manufacturer Sandoz, AG; and the policies of bustling Japanese corporations offer contrasts in management philosophy that might be eye-openers for American employers.

The average worker in German-speaking Basel arrives at work promptly at eight in the morning wearing a conservative suit, white shirt, and dark tie. But no one seems concerned when employees at Sandoz wander in shortly before nine wearing blue jeans and sweaters.

Sandoz's informality and flexible working hours are part of an overall program aimed at improving workers' morale and motivation. The program also seeks to remove status distinctions and allow everyone more freedom and say in decisions affecting their jobs.

All employees mix together in the same company restaurants, time clocks have been eliminated, all workers are paid on a monthly basis, and each employee participates in the process of determining his job description and performance rating.

Sandoz's employees now start work between 7 and 9 A.M. and finish between 4 and 7 P.M. Beyond that, they need only average eight and a half hours a day during one month. Credits or debits of ten hours can be carried from one month to the next.

"If I have a late night planned," explains Walter Suter, who works in the budgets department, "I tell my boss I will be in late the next morning. The important thing is that we do our eight hours and a half each day."

Production workers at Sandoz still work in shifts, but the plant has shifts beginning at 7, 7:30, and 8 in the morning and production line workers can choose which shift they wish to join. Once on it, they have to stick with it at least a month.

Sandoz officials say efficiency is up under the new plan and that labor turnover, which has a national industry average of 25 percent a year, has gone down to 12.4 percent. "Executives' work goes easier now too," says a top Sandoz official, "so we all derive a personal benefit."

Officials at Japan's Nihon Radiator Company, most of whom grew up under an even more stringent ethic than the Swiss-German philosophy of long hours and hard work, have taken a different tack in their search for greater efficiency and loyalty.

Nihon Radiator and a raft of other major Japanese corporations have taken to sending newly recruited executives to Self Defend Forces camps for several weeks of military training designed to develop an understanding of the hierarchical principal under which both military and corporate organizations operate.

During their time in uniform, Japanese corporate recruits drill, run assault courses, march 40 kilometers at a stretch, and learn how to salute, bow, stand at attention and give and take commands.

Since its inception in 1955, more than a million and a half Japanese civilians have participated in what has become known as the SDF Civilian Enrollment Program. At least half of the 100,000 civilians who now undergo the training every year, come from corporations.

Yoshiharu Nagao, manager of Nippon Univac Kaisha's personnel department, strongly believes that companies should assume responsibility for trying to reverse the trend toward permissiveness that educational authorities and parental control have allowed to develop.

"Japan's gross national product," contends Nagao, "is as high as it is today because of the way companies do things."

Japan Air Lines has sent nearly 5,000 people through military training since 1965 when the company's president announced that all employees would be required to take the course. Haruyuki Kuriyama, JAL education and training manager, says the company intends to instill a sense of team spirit and punctuality among new employees and to convey to them that the lazy days of campus life are over.

According to Kuriyama, "recruits who have finished the training say they feel wonderful and want others to share their experience with them." In fact the others have no choice but to share the experience, for at JAL—as with many Japanese corporations—no military indoctrinations, no job.

Isamu Sugimoto, an assistant general manager with the Izu-Hakone Railway confesses that "our managers are sent primarily to learn leadership and how to give commands. Of course," he is quick to add, "our company is not military-minded, but we think managers benefit greatly from this kind of training."

While the Japanese government has yet to point an accusing finger at companies who treat new employees to three all-expense-paid weeks in the country, Japan's Economic Planning Agency is showing concern about how the nation's male workers live their lives.

The average Japanese male, the Agency reports, works from young manhood to old age, uses his spare time to improve work skills and rarely takes either vacation or sick leave.

Since only 20 percent of Japanese workers actually take the paid vacations they are entitled to, because they are so accustomed to working *all* the time, they don't know what to do with the leisure.

The Japanese, states the Economic Agency's report, are so wrapped up in their work that they have little neighborhood or community consciousness. More seriously, the report concludes, they are working themselves to an early death.

The report of Japan's Economic Planning Agency didn't ask workers whether they were happy in their work, but if research conducted by Duke University's Center for the Study of Aging and Human Development is any indicator, the average Japanese worker may not be a happy man.

A 15-year study of 268 American working men, aged 60 to 94, convinced researchers that *work satisfaction,* and not hereditary factors as had long been believed, was the prime factor affecting longevity among the men studied. The number two factor found to extend the lives of subjects in the study was maintaining a "positive view of life." Third and fourth were "maintaining good physical functioning" and "avoid smoking."

How far American corporations will go to reduce the tensions and dissatisfactions of work, at executive, clerical, or blue-collar level, remains to be seen. For the time being, at least, breaking out may be the best course for many individuals who can't or won't wait any longer to take charge of their lives.

12

A Special Kind of Artist

A philosopher once said that, "Though painters and poets, sculptors and architects be honored among us, there is no artist so great as the teacher. His is the noblest medium of all and his works are the lives of those he has taught."

So it is with the men whose contributions form the next three chapters. Each is a special kind of teacher—a special kind of artist—and each is an outspoken and often criticized advocate of self-determination. The lives of Nicholas Johnson, Hal Lyon, and Sid Simon confirm that "breaking out" doesn't necessarily mean "dropping out."

Nicholas Johnson was Commissioner, Federal Communications Commission, 1966–73, and is the author of *How to Talk Back to Your Television Set* (Little, Brown; and Bantam, 1970) and *Test Pattern for Living* (Bantam, 1972), from which Chapter Fourteen is drawn.

Hal Lyon, Ph.D., is Director of Education for the

Gifted and Talented, U.S. Department of Health, Education and Welfare, a post he "stepped down to," after resigning as Deputy Associate Commissioner for Education. He is a West Point graduate, former Vietnam paratrooper-ranger-combat commander. He is the author of *Learning to Feel, Feeling to Learn* (Merrill).

Sid Simon, also a Ph.D., is professor of humanistic education at the University of Massachusetts. A widely published author, he has written two volumes of children's stories, *Henry: The Uncatchable Mouse* and *The Armadillo Without A Shell* (both published by W. W. Norton). His most recent book is: *Values Clarification: A Practical Handbook for Teachers and Students* (Hart).

Although Nicholas Johnson, Hal Lyon, and Sid Simon have all changed the system in important ways, their concern, it seems to me, is more that people discover themselves and in doing that, discover their own ways of breaking out.

If their writing on these pages has anything in common, it is perhaps their agreement with Galileo, who felt that, "You cannot teach a man anything; you can only help him find it within himself."

13

Discovering Myself

by HALLYON

I originally contacted Hal Lyon because a friend told me he would soon be breaking out. Dr. Lyon, my informant reported, was a high government official who had turned in his resignation and was going off to live on a lake somewhere in New Hampshire.

When I met Hal in his GS–18 "supergrade" office in Washington I learned that my information was only partly correct. Hal was getting out of the rat race all right, but he was hardly moving across the street to do it. As for the lake in New Hampshire, it was a nice place to visit, but he wouldn't want to live there.

But Hal had submitted his resignation as Deputy Associate Commissioner for Education, stepping several rungs down the ladder to become Director of Education for the Gifted and Talented.

By moving into H. E. W.'s educational program for the gifted, Hal Lyon was moving into exactly what he wanted to do. But although his new position was far from menial, he'd had to resist the pressures of coworkers who urged him not to step down to a position of "lesser" importance. His battle was within himself too, for, if anything, Hal Lyon had always been an achiever. He had never taken a step backward in his life.

"In taking that step backward," he told me, "I probably took the biggest step forward in my entire life because in stepping down I finally turned in the rule book that says we have to live by other people's values and started living by my own."

Talking with Hal Lyon as he smoothly dealt with whatever responsibilities of his job came through his office door, and, a few days later, seated on the floor at dinner with his wife and children, I came to feel that what Hal had to impart for this book deserved to be related fully and could much better be said by Hal than by me.

During the weeks following our interviews Hal and I spoke by telephone several times about his writing something "for the book," but there was never time. Of course, he finally agreed and "Discovering Myself" is what he wrote about his own "breaking out."

Hardly sounding at all like the West Point graduate he is, and former perfectionist he used to be, Hal Lyon writes, "I believe that what's beautiful about people is not perfectionism, but our flaws and vulnerabilities. Hothouse vegetables grown in a protected way don't seem to have nearly the flavor of vegetables that are exposed to the wind and the rain. The same seems to be true with people. Perfectionism isn't what's beautiful. What's beautiful is our humanism, which means we are real."

Hal Lyon

When a former combat-type military officer writes about getting in touch with personal feelings and individual goals with a view toward "breaking out," the reader deserves an explanation. I spent four years at West Point being educated and conditioned to be a professional soldier. The West Point years were followed by Ranger and paratrooper training, working for General Westmoreland setting up a counterguerilla school, and commanding a rifle company in the 101st Airborne Division in Viet Nam.

Though I learned many lessons during that time, those were years in which I also learned to deny my personal desires and natural inclinations in order to earn rewards for attainment of goals set by society.

While at Esalen Institute a few years ago I went down to the baths early one morning—a beautiful place, set into the cliffs at Big Sur, high above the Pacific. I was sitting there looking out at the ocean and I thought, "the ocean is so beautiful, and yet it's bad." The ocean lashes at the shorelines and drowns people and turns over ships. Yet in its wisdom, it doesn't worry about its badness, it's just there.

And next I thought, "Perhaps I'm beautiful too, even with my 'badness.' " Now, I had spent the past few years realizing that I was beautiful *with* all my accomplishments. To be beautiful without the achievements was something else. I thought, "What if I stripped off my title as Deputy Associate Commissioner of Education? I'd still be beautiful without that. What if I hadn't written my book? I'd still be beautiful." And I was thinking of symbolically throwing my book off the cliff until I realized that it wasn't the book that was bad. It was my *need* for it that was my problem.

I went on, stripping away my Ph.D., graduation from West Point and all my accomplishments all the way back to making the high-school football team when I weighed fifty pounds less than the other kids. I hadn't known until then that I'd spent years working for someone else's goals instead of my own. I hadn't been in charge of my life.

During that same visit to Esalen, I tripped back to an event when I was five years old. I was in a train station in Boston and my father was there in his World War II army uniform with a duffel bag and my mother was crying. I heard the steam coming out of the locomotive, and my father put his hand on my shoulder and said, "You're the man of the house now. Take care of your mom. You be good and I'll hurry home." That "You be good and I'll hurry home" stuck in my mind and I tried so hard to be good, but he didn't come home for three years. I tried harder and harder and I just knew I wasn't good enough. I think that's when I first became the overachiever, trying to chalk up all those accomplishments in order to be accepted for them. But what I really wanted was for my father to "come home." I suspect that's how many of us became overachievers.

Just after I recalled the scene with my father I was lying on a wet massage table at the baths and all of a sudden I was a baby in my crib. I was wet and, "Bad baby, bad baby" was going through my head. Someone must have said I was bad for wetting my crib! When I became aware of this I thought, "That's not bad, that's beautiful!" and I heard the wretched, wet baby I'd been, who was beautiful even without all those accomplishments—not needing those.

I believe that what's beautiful about people is not perfectionism, but our flaws and vulnerabilities. Hothouse vegetables grown in a protected way don't seem to have nearly the flavor of vegetables that are grown outside where they are exposed to the wind and the rain and the weather. The same seems to be true with people.

People who are overprotected—or who try to be "perfect"—are just not as colorful. Who wants a perfect spouse or a perfect lover? Who wants to have grown up with a perfect brother or sister and perfect mother and father? Perfectionism isn't what's beautiful. What's beautiful is our humanism, our vulnerability which means we are real.

The key learning experiences of my life have come, not from school or other formal learning situations, but rather from personal crises and experiences in dealing with life. I wrote my book *Learning to Feel, Feeling to Learn* (Charles E. Merrill, 1971), for example, during a time of intense loneliness.

I had just split with my first wife after ten years of marriage. I went to a lake in New Hampshire where I'd spent most of my childhood summers. My two boys were with me, but otherwise I was quite alone. Whenever I had been lonely in the past, I had gathered friends around me or made myself busy "accomplishing" things to evade the loneliness. This was a time when I didn't quite want to outrun it; I let it catch up with me. I had been running for most of my life and never admitting to myself that I could be lonely, so I got very deeply into my loneliness and spent a lot of time crying—something else I'd never done before.

I found that loneliness is a very positive kind of emotion to deal with. Beneath my veneer of toughness was all kinds of new creativity and a lot of new strength. Even more important for me was a new-found tenderness—a little-boy part that grew up at age five—a part that West Point never nourished. I believe that behind most of our emotions, loneliness, anger, or whatever, there is an important part of us that we need to experience totally. To the extent that we deny the existence of those feelings, we live a fraction of our potential.

When I look back at my activity-filled life, it's almost

as though I had to fill each day and weekend with spectacular, special activities. People do this, I'm convinced,
when they feel there is nothing spectacular or special
inside themselves or between themselves and others. For
many years I had so filled my life with superevents that
I had "tuned out" the people I was close to but not really
with. Not long ago I had an experience that is a perfect
example of "tuning people out."

I was in a Columbia University conference, a meeting
that included the University's trustees, key administrators, faculty and key student leaders, and a group of
outsiders. We gathered at Arden House, a country estate
north of New York City. Dr. Carl Rogers and a team of
encounter-group leaders were called in at the last minute
in an attempt to open up communications between the
various University factions.

Early in the conference Carl Rogers organized us into
several encounter groups. Before long, one of the faculty
members in our group began to slide his chair farther
and farther back from the circle, and after a while Dr.
Rogers said, "I have the feeling you're trying to with-
draw from this group. Is that true?" And the faculty
member said, "You're darned right I'm trying to with-
draw from this group! I didn't come here to be psycho-
analyzed! I came here to learn. Learning takes place on
an intellectual level and I haven't heard a wise intellectual statement uttered yet. Anybody that would really
like to do some learning," he continued, "is invited to go
into the next room where we can try to get to the root
of the crisis at Columbia on an intellectual level."

The president of a major foundation was in our group
and said, "Now I'm beginning to understand what happened at Columbia." And a student jumped up and said,

"That's exactly it! Every time we try to be real human beings dealing with *feelings* and *emotions,* this is the kind of response we get. They won't deal on any level but the *intellectual* level. And we can't challenge them there. They're the world's living experts!"

A little later on we were down in a large conference hall, with the whole group assembled, and the students asked for an hour to try to bridge the communications gap they felt existed between them and the administration and faculty. (The president of Columbia, interestingly, had said the one thing they didn't have at Columbia was a communication problem.)

The students were showing great emotion and one student, with tears running down his face, after trying for twenty minutes to relate to the faculty and administration, finally came up to the president of Columbia and said, "Take off your presidency, just for a moment. Show me there's a human being underneath! Admit you've made a mistake just once in your life!" The president cleared his throat, "Ah hum, it's not my policy to . . ." and the student said, "Fuck your policy!"

This was a student with a "Jesus Saves" T-shirt and hair down to his shoulders, a very articulate student who quoted the Bible and other sources in literature, beautifully threading his citations through the comments he was making. He turned to the people there and said, "It all boils down to a dichotomy of feeling versus intellect, or, to put it another way, morality versus duplicity!" and he sat down.

A faculty member popped up and started to lecture. A Harvard psychologist interrupted and said, "Just a minute. I don't think many of you heard what the student said. It was a very wise thing. He said that faculty members, on their intellectual planes, are safe there and they can't be challenged, and that students see that as duplicity since they are dealing with their intellectual side. The students see themselves struggling with their *feelings* as well as their intellects, and they see that as moral. It is moral to be dealing with your whole self rather than practicing duplicity or being one-dimensional half-men. So that is the crux of the problem at Columbia and at universities throughout this country."

Before I left that conference I began to realize that all around the country we have many one-dimensional half-men, brilliantly developed intellectually, but often stunted emotionally. Many of these people teaching in classrooms and running many of our biggest corporations, are afraid to deal with feelings, the side of man that makes him human.

People who feel frustrated and undernourished within the educational and corporate systems are really victims of emotional deficiency in their life diets. We've long known that when people suffer from a vitamin deficiency they develop a craving for whatever will satisfy that deprivation.

Many kids who are dropping out of school are doing so out of frustration with education's lack of relevance to their *whole* lives, lives that include emotions and feelings as well as intellectual thoughts. Others are leaving the corporate system for the same reasons: the absence of an opportunity, within that system, to be intellectual *and* emotional—to be whole men.

I'm convinced that if we can deal with the whole man in the classroom, if teachers can begin to deal with children as *feeling* human beings instead of just intellectuals to be developed, then there is hope for education in this country. And if corporate leaders begin to deal with each other and the public as human beings with feelings, fewer of our most sensitive, moral, and creative people will find it necessary to leave industry in self-defense. Until that happens, however, there is no alternative for many people exept to "get out."

The president at Columbia, who was begged to "Take off your presidency, just for a moment," and many of our school officials and business leaders are trapped by their roles. The more they—and we—are "into" our roles as teachers, or businessmen, or students or even parents, the more we separate ourselves from people around us.

A couple of summers ago, I met Baba Ram Dass (once known as Richard Alpert). He was a Ph.D., professor at Harvard, a pilot, a cellist, an author of several books, a lecturer, and a psychotherapist. Discovering that this wasn't enough, he left all of this and went to Esalen for a year, followed by a year and a half in India with a guru. Baba Ram Dass is one of the wisest and most spiritual men I have ever known.

As Ram Dass and I were talking together, I could feel us telescoping closer together, then farther apart, then closer. I told him I could feel this, and he said, "To the extent that we wear masks and play roles, distance comes between us. To the extent that we are two human beings with one another, we are closer."

He suggested that when we were getting farther apart, he was probably playing guru, or I was playing Dr. Lyon or Deputy Associate Commissioner or some other such role. And when we got closer together, we were two human beings digging each other. We talked about getting out of our roles and he said, "Try this with your children."

It's hard to take off my father role. I look at my children, of course, usually with lots of love (except when I'm angry). But it's hard to take owl that evaluative father role. I called my son Gregg over and took off my father role and looked into his eyes. What a really beautiful human being he is! I saw him in a new light and he could feel me feeling this and I could feel him recognizing it, and we found in each other's eyes a warm peak moment of joy and beauty.

I'm discovering a lot of things now that I didn't see earlier. Though I'm still working for the same government agency, I've left my more bureaucratic job as Deputy Associate Commissioner to develop an educational program for gifted children.

Getting in touch with my loneliness, and discovering at Esalen just where some of my drives to overachieve were coming from, taught me a lot of things I never realized before. I had been numb for thirty-three years! When you compare your life to the longevity of a star—it's just a spark and it's over with. It's so important when you realize this, to be vital and not numb. And that means dealing with emotions and feelings, the essence of *you* that's behind your emotions, instead of constraining your ego boundaries—instead of having a set of predictable, fixed responses imposed by the roles you have been conditioned to play. We realize only five to fifteen percent of our potential in our lifetime. Yet to the degree we can be spontaneous—here and now—reacting to what happens at the moment, we have most of our potential available. Yet few schools, few institutions encourage such spontaneity. Most encourage a fixed, predictable set of responses—and society calls this "character."

If you are caught in a system that imposes straight-jacket roles that make being "you" an almost impossible thing to do, perhaps getting out of the system is a step toward discovering yourself. A freeing step from environmental support to self-support, but also a step toward getting your approval from within yourself and a step away from being a slave to what everyone else expects you to be.

14

*Writing Your Own Script**

by NICHOLAS JOHNSON

Trying to catch former Federal Communications Commissioner Nicholas Johnson gave me a pretty good idea of what it's like being a slow fox trying to bag that cartoon character, Road Runner. I saw him three times before we talked, twice disappearing rapidly down the corridors of the FCC's Washington, D.C. headquarters, and once relatively at rest in his reception room as he and a couple of his aides watched some crucial Congressional hearings on television.

I guess you'd have to call his offices mod, as mod as a government office can be anyway. And every time I was on the floor where Commissioners have their suites, his was the only door that was open.

His staff was young and the very sharp legal aide I got to know arranging and rearranging appointments to see Mr. Johnson could have gone underground and vanished instantly in Washington's left-bank Georgetown district merely by removing his tie. Come to think of it, so could Commissioner Johnson.

Even before the Nixon administration, long-haired, bicycle-riding Commissioner Johnson earned the epithet, "the President's (Lyndon Johnson's) maverick in the FCC." It would be safe to

---

*From *Test Pattern for Living*, copyright 1972 by Nicholas Johnson.

say that Commissioner Johnson became the man radio and televi-
sion network officials would have most liked to drop from the
highest antenna tower they could find.

What other FCC Commissioner would tell the public to spend
more time outside watching sunsets and less time listening to the
radio and watching TV?

Nicholas Johnson is another one of those people who feel in-
dividuals can figuratively shake their fists at the system, start
living on their own terms, and get away with it. He does, and he's
got something to say about how other people can do it too.

So I didn't seek out Commissioner Johnson because I'd heard
he was someone who was getting out of the rat race. I'd read a
few things he'd written and wanted to include his words on these
pages because I thought they made sense for anyone who felt he
had some breaking out of his own to do.

Not everything he says here is new. Some of his ideas he's
included in books and magazine articles or speeches, as well as our
two interviews—mostly conducted at a fast walk through his
offices, in and out of the men's room, and up and down the halls
of the FCC building where for all his turbulent ways he still
managed to win friends and influence a lot of people.

The former Honorable Commissioner also asks a lot of ques-
tions, among them: "How about trying to find out what you would
do and be if there wasn't some corporation trying to sell you on
doing everything its way?"

Nicholas Johnson

I see evidence all around me that people are rejecting
materialism and looking for more meaningful lives for
themselves. Housewives, executives, blue-collar workers
and farmers, not just intellectuals, college students, radi-

cals and professors, are taking *action* in their daily lives
that supports what the theorists have been saying all
along about the inhumanity of the corporate consumption standard.

Ordinary people, by the thousands, without the internal or external direction of an ideology or an operating
manual are, in a violent spasm of reaction, simply casting
off the chains of corporate control of their lives. The
point is not that I find this encouraging—although I do.
Or even that I think the system may, after all, be capable
of righting itself. The point is that the actions of all these
people are simply additional evidence that the corporate
life is, like war, unhealthy for children and other living
things.

Anyone looking at our society today immediately un-
covers some very troubling statistical reports—"indicia
of social disintegration."

—The number of patients in mental hospitals and psy-
  chiatric outpatient clinics has increased 50 percent
  in the last ten years.
—The per capita consumption of alcohol has been
  rising since 1950; alcoholism is by all odds the nation's number one hard-drug problem.
—The number of unwanted illegitimate births per
  thousand has nearly quadrupled since 1940.
—Juvenile delinquency cases per thousand population
  have nearly tripled since 1950.
—The divorce rate has risen steadily since 1940, running as high as 70 percent in some West Coast communities.
—Suicide now ranks as the fifth leading cause of death
  among fifteen- to twenty-four-year-olds.
—Two years ago a Harris poll indicated that 28 per-

cent of the adult population—more than 33 million
Americans—felt substantially alienated from the
mainstream of American society.

These figures—to which more could be added—can be
variously interpreted. None alone "proves" anything.
But, taken together, they provide some hard evidence
that a great many Americans are showing the strain, and
a reasonable basis for suspecting that a great many more
of us are feeling pressures that show up in lesser ways.

"O.K., what's my alternative?" you ask.

"How about life?" How about trying to find out what
you would do, and be, and think, and create if there
wasn't some corporation trying to sell you on doing it all
their way.

But just how would you go about that? It's heady stuff
to lie on the grass and gaze at the clouds, but how about
the 99.99 percent of the American people who can't do
that?

Suppose you don't want to drop out or camp out.
Maybe you want to step in, try to make things a little
better, or just earn a living. What then? How can we
make our lives more liveable and more human? You
cannot "buy" or "sell" a new identity. You cannot just
walk into a nonconformist store and buy the latest nonconformist clothes, records, and wall posters and get it
over with. Those businessmen who have tried have made
few profits or prophets.

Because what we are really talking about is a rebirth of
the human personality. We are talking about a blend of
philosophy, psychiatry, politics and poetry that must be
personally experienced and worked through. You not
only can't buy the finished product, you can't even buy
a kit and assemble it yourself.

Indeed, central to this renaissance of the human spirit is a self-determination, power, and simplicity that is totally at odds with the purchase of most of the products sold, for example, in a typical, large urban all-purpose "drug store."

Why buy kitchen cleansers, toothpaste, mouthwash, bath salts, room freshener, burn ointments, children's clay, and stomach settlers—for many dollars—when you can get it all in a little box of Arm and Hammer bicarbonate of soda for pennies?

Or take the matter of bicycle riding. You don't ride a bicycle because you hate General Motors but lack the courage to bomb an auto plant. You don't do it as a gesture of great stoicism and personal sacrifice. You are not even engaged, necessarily, in an act of political protest over the company's responsibility for most of the air pollution (by tonnage) in the United States. It's like finally giving up cigarettes. You just wake up one morning and realize you don't want to start the day with another automobile. Just as cigarette smoking is not a pleasure, it's a business; so you finally come to realize that you don't need General Motors, they need you. They need you to drive their cars for them. You are driving for Detroit, and paying them to do it. Automobiles are just a part of your life that's over, that's all. No hard feelings. You've just moved on to something else. From now on you just use their buses, taxis, and rental cars when they suit your convenience. You don't keep one for them that you have to house, feed and water, and care for.

I ride a bicycle because I enjoy it more than driving a car. It makes me *feel* better. It is always good exercise. It gets your lungs to breathing and your heart to pumping. Dr. Paul Dudley White and others have long advised it

as a means of warding off heart attacks. If you can use a
bicycle to get to and from work, you can have the added
satisfaction of knowing that you are providing a life support activity for yourself: transportation. In my case, I
bicycle along the C & O Canal tow path in Washington,
D.C., where I live, so it also provides me daily time in a
natural setting with canal, river, trees, birds, changing
seasons, and sky. I find this time especially good for
doing some of my best thinking, something I found very
difficult to do during an earlier phase when I was jog-
ging. So it also serves as a time when I compose little
poems and songs, think of ideas for opinions and
speeches, and think about matters philosophical.

On those occasions when I am not able to cycle along
the canal—because it is rough with ice, or muddy from
rain or melting snow—bicycling enables me to keep
closer to the street people: folks waiting for buses or to
cross streets, street sweepers, policemen, men unloading
trucks, and so forth. Needless to say, I cannot claim any
depth of understanding as a result of such momentary
and chance encounters, but I do somewhat have the
sense—by the time I get to the office—that I have a much
better feeling for the mood of the city that day than the
public officials who have come to their offices in limou-
sines or their own automobiles.

So you can start looking around for simplifications,
ways to make you less possession-bound and give you
more chance to participate in your life. The opportunities are endless. Start by searching your house or apartment for things you can throw away. Ask yourself, "If I
were living in the woods, would I spend a day going to
town to buy this aerosol can?" Look for simple substitutes.

Look for unnecessary electrical and other machinery and appliances. Bread can be toasted in the broiler of the stove. Carving knives and toothbrushes really need not be electrically powered. Put fruit and vegetable waste in a compost heap instead of down an electric disposal. I took up shaving with a blade, brush, and shaving soap instead of an electric razor. It's kind of bloody, but it's more fun.

You can easily ignore most of the products in your supermarket and do a little more food preparation from basic ingredients yourself. But I'm not interested in giving cooking or any other of these activities a lot of time.

I'll walk up to a mile in dense urban areas because I can move faster that way than in a car—as well as get exercise, not pollute, help fight the automotive life-style, save money, and do a "life thing," transporting myself, naturally.

In an industrialized urban environment it is easy to forget that human life still is, as it was originally, sustained by some of these basic functions. I think *some* participation in the support of your life is essential to a sense of fulfillment. And yet I used to give almost no attention to these kinds of activities. Food simply appeared on my dinner table ready to eat. The house I lived in was purchased. It was warmed or cooled by some equipment in the basement that I knew very little about, and was tended to by repairmen when necessary. Clothing was something that I found in closets and dresser drawers, and was cleaned and mended by my wife, or the maid, or a cleaning establishment. Transportation was provided by the municipal bus system for commuting, and by FCC drivers during the day. At my office I was not only surrounded by machinery—copying machines, electric typewriters, dictating machines, and so forth—but also by people paid to operate them for me, answer my telephone, and bring me coffee.

I had, in short, taken very nearly all my life support activities—"my life"—and cut them up into bits and pieces which I parceled out to individuals, corporations, and machines around me. The upshot was that there was very little of it left for me to live. This was extraordinarily "efficient" in one sense. That is, I was working at perhaps 98 percent of the ultimate level of professional production of which I am capable. But what I concluded was that it was bad for life. For I was *living* only a small percentage of my ultimate capacity to live.

If you see some similarities to your own life—or what your own life will likely become—the question is what to do about it.

Find those places where you can break through the interlocked system now and get some of those bits and pieces of your life back that you are paying other people to live for you. Bicycle riding may be totally impractical for you. O.K., then find something else. Raise some of your own food. Make some of your own clothes. You can't possibly do it all, and wouldn't want to. There would be no time left to read and write poetry.

As I said, you don't have to do it all, but you can do enough of it to regain the feeling that it's your life you're living. You do need to know that you are only consuming because *you* need to and want to, not because the big corporations need for you to.

The problem is that our nonlife in the corporate state does get interlocked: business suits, automobiles, air-conditioning, restaurants, underarm deodorant, cocktail parties, suburban homes, and television watching are kind of interdependent. Once you get a big house you fill it full of things—more things than you "need" or even enjoy. Then you need other things to take care of those things, and a station wagon to haul them, and a repairman to fix them, and so on ad infinitum.

I think most grown men and women need to have a sense that they are capable of, and are involved in some kind of productivity that is paid for, or otherwise generally recognized as a value to society. The problem, of course, is that it is all too easy for such activities to consume virtually *all* of your intellectual, emotional, and physical energy—as they had for me.

So I began to think about the other basic elements of life. If I were to plan an ideal day for human life, what would it contain?

Most fundamental, I suppose, is love. Each of us has different feelings and relationships we have thought of as love. Sexuality can be an important part of it. Each of us means something a little different by it. But we would probably all agree that

> Oh, to exist
> Is very nice
> But scarcely half as fine
> As with the love
> And other stuff
> That makes it just divine

And we would probably also agree that there's very little more I should or need contribute at this point to the thousands of volumes, poems, and songs on that subject.

Contemplation of some kind has been considered fundamental by man throughout the ages. I decided to include it as another basic element. It can be "religion," philoso-

phy, mythology, yoga, or whatever makes sense for you.
But we have to have some time when we think beyond
our hangnails and hangovers to a somewhat more meaningful view of life than the daily routine.

Personal analysis is a related activity. Psychiatrists or
counseling services or encounter groups are one way to
do it. But thinking to oneself, writing in a journal, or
regularly talking with a trusted friend are other ways to
achieve related benefits. Most of us could do with a little
more knowledge about why we tick the way we do.

The journal should be bound. I formerly jotted things
on sheets of yellow pads. It's not a "diary." It's a sketch
book, a workbook for life. It's poems, recipes, love notes,
furniture designs, speech drafts, silly thoughts, serious
reflections, and drawings, all mixed together, like life is
—or should be. It's a tangible record of the balance in
your life. It makes you see better, take life with both
more seriousness and more whimsy. I like it.

Creative expression, the opportunity to *be* creative—personally, not just professionally—as well as being exposed
to beauty and the best creativity of others is essential to
individual growth.

Creativity is an essential quality of humanness in two
respects. First, as Emerson suggested, "If the man cre-
ates not, the pure efflux of the Deity is not his—cinders
and smoke there may be, but not the flame." Creativity
means, by definition, that which makes man, and each
man, unique. If a person is to have his own individuality,
his own unique self, it will be expressed in creative and
artistic ways most honestly and fully. If you do not give
yourself the opportunity to be creative, you are, in a very
meaningful sense, depriving yourself of the opportunity
to be human.

Regular contact with nature is a necessary reminder of the whole earth system from which we came, in which we live, and to which we will return. Living in the woods may or may not be the best way to keep in touch with our origins.

Whether or not you end up permanently leaving the city to live in the woods, a natural environment is a good place to sort out the basics of living.

I have always enjoyed hiking and camping so the West Virginia mountains seemed the best setting for my own odyssey.

For two weeks my two young sons and I lived on some isolated forestland and those two weeks reaffirmed my latent but basic commitment to the psychic values of simplicity. You not only can get along with substantially fewer "things" when camping, you actually enjoy life more because it is not so cluttered with objects.

The experience gave me a way of thinking about simplicity, objects, and natural living that I had not had before.

Whether the truths I am dealing with are biological or metaphysical, my own experience supports the lessons of the world's great teachers. If man is to develop the rich individuality and full potential of which he is capable he needs more than the hollow values and products of consumerism. He needs not only productive "work," but also love, beauty, creativity, contemplation, contact with nature, and participation in the support of his own life. When we live our lives in ways that take us too far from those basic truths, we begin to find ourselves in all kinds of troubles that ultimately show up in social statistics. And the evidence seems to suggest that as we return to a richer and more natural life, our problems seem to subside. Whether or not that is enough for you, it is enough for me.

Central to all that I suggest is the necessity that you work it out for *yourself*. *You* need to discover who you are, what feels right and best for *you*. You not only need to walk to the sound of a different drummer, you need to be that different drummer. You need to write your own music. You need to look inside yourself and see what is there. I think some time in the woods is useful for this purpose. But camping may not make sense for you, for a variety of quite sensible reasons. That's fine. The purpose of self-discovery is not to stop copying Howard Johnson and start copying Nick Johnson—or anybody else. The point is to find your own soul and kick it, and poke it with a stick, see if it's still alive, and then watch which way it moves.

15

Star Trek

by SIDNEY B. SIMON

I never met Sid Simon. We tried, but his lecture and consulting travel, plus my own wide-ranging interviews for this book never allowed us to be in the same place at the same time. By the time this book appears, we'll probably have managed a meeting someplace. I hope so anyway.

There were things I kept hearing about Sid from mutual friends that made me think he might be a good man to talk to. For one thing, he was doing exactly what he wanted to, so in a sense he was, like Nicholas Johnson and Hal Lyon, out of the rat race. Perhaps, I thought, he could look back from the perspective of one who had once been there.

But there were other things I kept hearing that made me think Sid was the kind of person readers would like to meet.

"In Sid's family," a mutual acquaintance told me, "whenever someone drops something, if someone else is in the room, they pick it up for them. Or if he breaks an egg, say, or spills a glass of water, someone else cleans it up." That's a nice value to have, I thought, especially as in Sid's house, where family relationships are not tied to child-parent roles.

"Christmas morning at the Simons'," someone else reported,

"begins with the youngest child going to the tree and getting the presents he has made (not purchased), and taking them one by one to each member of the family to open while the giver tells how he came to make that particular gift for each, and what it means to him.

"This is followed by the next youngest and so on up until sometime during the evening, after breaks for meals, when father's turn to give his gifts comes."

Finally, I wanted to include Sid Simon's wisdom on these pages because he is a pro. His responsibilities as professor of Humanistic Education at the University of Massachusetts and his work as consultant to educational institutions centers on what psychologists call "values clarification," helping individuals discover what their personal values really are.

In Dr. Simon's work as cartographer of the emotions and intellect there are no "shoulds" and "should nots" when it comes to personal values. "Each person's values, like his mind and body," he says, "are his own."

Dr. Simon has conducted values clarification workshops and seminars at nearly every major university in the United States and for many of America's leading corporations. Not surprisingly, participants in many programs Sid had conducted discovered for the first time they were sacrificing the satisfactions of values one through five or six to pay for attainment of a value that turned out to be far down on their list.

In putting together "Star Trek" for readers of this book, Dr. Simon set down for the first time in writing some of the guidelines he has followed in his personal work with people who were looking for a way out.

Sidney B. Simon

You don't have to be a philosopher to be concerned about values. You've probably done some thinking about your own values lately, especially if you're thinking about "breaking out" or "staying in."

Values are the stars by which men steer their lives, guide their choices and give viability to their search for meaning. The tricky thing is that there is no one set of right answers for all people.

I would like to take you on a short values-clarifying journey with me. I think it could help sort out some things which make decisions about changing our lives so confusing and full of conflict.

Get a piece of paper and number down the middle, 1 through 20. (This is NOT a test. Each item will NOT be worth five points.) Better yet, you won't be asked to share this list with anyone. It is your private search. Really, if you can't find the time to do this exercise now, don't read on. Come back to it, because doing the 1–20 listing right will just make a lot of things about your values more clear.

O.K., now what do you list? Simply put down twenty things in life that you really LOVE TO DO. Yes, any twenty things at all, and the only requirement is that you truly love to do it. (No fair listing the same lovely thing twenty times.) Put down twenty different things in your life which you love to do.

Now that you've listed your twenty things you love to do, *code* your list in the following ways:

1. Put a $ (dollar) sign next to every item that requires an expenditure of at least $5 every time you do it.

(Don't count the money it costs to buy the equipment. For example, if you were into bike riding, you wouldn't put a dollar sign in front of it even though your bike cost more than $5. The issue here is that it costs you $5 *each* time you do it.)

2. Use the letters A (for alone), P (for people), and S (for a special person) and record which is your preference. For each activity, do you PREFER to do it alone, or with people, or with some special person? (Not necessarily the same special person for each activity.) Note that you can often do a certain activity alone or with people or with a special person. The coding here, however, records your *preference*.

3. Put an R next to every item that has an element of *risk* to it. It can be physical risk or emotional risk or intellectual risk. It doesn't have to be risky for anyone else. Just get in touch with which of your twenty loves are risky for you.

4. Think of someone you love. Place an X in front of every item on your list which you hope would appear on his or her list if he or she had made a list of twenty loves, also. (In fact, you might want to get that person to do just such a thing. It could form a very significant data bank for both of you as you consider this decision to leave or to stay.)

5. Place the number 10 next to any item that probably would not have been on your list ten years ago.

6. Place a 5 next to anything you love to do which you think might not remain on your list five years from now.

7. Finally, date each item to show when you did it last. You need not be perfectly accurate. It is O.K. to say something like, "During August of 1971."

There are many ways to look at the data generated by the twenty-loves list, but one of the simplest and most effective things we've found to do with this exercise (and many of the other values exercises, as well) is to write down or say to someone you trust a series of "I learned's."

"I learned's" are sentences that always have two first-person pronouns in them. Here are some examples:

I LEARNED'S

I learned that I. . . .
I re-learned that I. . . .
I see that I need to. . . .
I was disappointed to notice that I. . . .
I feel ready to affirm that I. . . .
It surprised the hell out of me to see that I. . . .

Putting together a series of "I learned's" often makes the exercise take on a real change agent role. Some of our students report that it is the first time they ever saw so clearly how sweet life can be. We always get reminded, too, of that line out of *Auntie Mame*—"Life is a banquet and most bastards are starving to death."

Another exercise that could help all of us get clearer on where we stand on some of the issues that influence our decision to stay or to break out. We call it the Weekly Reaction Sheet.

Get some sheets of carbon paper and type off four of the following sheets. Then, once a week, say, on Sunday night, answer the questions and put the sheet aside. After you've done them for four weeks, spread them on a table and make some "I learned's" from the data that leaps out at you from your four weekly-reaction sheets.

WEEKLY REACTION SHEET

Date_____

1. What was the highpoint of this week for you? Think about the second highpoint, and what made the *real* highpoint win?

2. With whom were you in emphatic agreement or dis- agreement this week?

3. Did you make any plans for some future happening? Make any dates, order any tickets, invite someone to join you on anything, etc.?

4. What did you procrastinate about this week?

5. In what ways could the week have been better?

6. With whom do you have any unfinished business this week?

Like so many of the values-clarification exercises, this weekly reaction builds its impact slowly and steadily. Just facing four weeks of our life, and thinking about what we really seek for our high points is almost worth the trip. But to also get in touch with those people with whom we are in agreement or disagreement, and notice that word "emphatic," is often a revelation. So it is with the other questions, we have found.

By now you are either intrigued or perhaps turned off to this way of systematically examining the values we use in making our everyday choices. If you are still with me, let me show you a simple strategy that has many different possible applications. We call it Baker's Dozen. Here's the way it goes.

For a starter, simply list thirteen things you use with some frequency that have plugs. That is, thirteen things drawing electricity that you use regularly. You might list your shaver and the toaster, etc. But think of some that mean something to you, and not necessarily to the whole family. Here you might mention the electric drill, or your slide projector, or the adding machine at the office, or the ubiquitous Xerox machine.

Now, imagine that there has been a declaration of a serious power shortage, and you have to give up five of the thirteen appliances on the list. Draw a line through the five you would be willing to give up first.

Then draw a line through five more that you could live without. Or, you could approach it from the other end and circle the three items with plugs that you would hold on to down to the bitter end. These are the three you consider most precious from the whole list of thirteen.

That's the way Baker's Dozen works. Now, think of some other applications.

Other Issues for the Bakers's Dozen

1. List thirteen things you now have to do on your present job. These are thirteen tasks that usually demand your attention. (Answering the mail, end-of-month expense reports, etc.) Draw a line through the five that you dislike the most. Circle the three that are the nicest parts of the job.

2. Jot down thirteen places where you might want to vacation sometime. Draw a line through five that you wouldn't cry too much over if you never got there. Circle three that you might be unhappy about if you don't vacation there someday.

3. List thirteen books you've been trying to find time to read. Draw a line through five that wouldn't be such a loss if you never got to them, and circle three that seem precious to you.

4. Do the same with thirteen movies.

5.   Or thirteen letters you need to answer.
6.   Or thirteen phone calls it might be nice to make.
7.   Or thirteen people you've been meaning to go visit.

I think you get the idea.

I want to make it clear that there is a sound theoretical framework to all of this work in values clarification. In simplest terms, values can be examined via seven separate processes. These processes become the criteria for our definition of a value, which is anything that meets all *seven* criteria. Anything that clears six or five or less criteria we call a VALUE-INDICATOR. Words that are not quite regal enough to be called *values,* but that have a lot of value-laden qualities, are value-indicator words, such as attitudes, beliefs, feelings, thoughts, morals, aspirations, goals, etc. Once you begin working with values-clarification, your effort begins to lift a value-indicator to the level of a value.

You lift it by working on the criteria previously not sufficiently examined. Here are the criteria, and then I'd like to take us back to our twenty-loves list to try and see which of those were values and which were value-indicators.

The Seven Criteria of Processes for a Value
Before something can be a value, it must be:
1.   Prized and cherished
2.   Part of a pattern, that is, repeated with some consistency
3.   Chosen from among alternatives
4.   Freely chosen
5.   Chosen after due reflection
6.   Publicly affirmed
7.   Acted upon

These are demanding criteria. Most people have very few values, though they may have a number of value-indicators. People with very *few* values tend to be conforming, apathetic, inconsistent, ambivalent, alienated, frenzied, overworked, and hassled, all of which seems quite logical when you realize the extent to which values guide a man's life.

If you refer back to your twenty-loves list, you can examine those items to see which are *values* and which are more appropriately called value-*indicators*. It's just a matter of running each love-list selection down the seven criteria above. You can do it by asking yourself a series of questions:

Do I really prize and cherish this item? (Golf, or eating gourmet dinners, or making love, etc.)

Can I recognize it as part of a pattern that I make time for, consistently, and build into my life often enough so I can really see its presence in my life?

Did I choose it from a number of alternatives? (If it was golf, for example, did I also consider squash, badminton, handball, ice hockey, etc., etc., etc.)

Did I choose it without pressure, freely and after a lot of hard thinking?

Now we come to a most interesting criterion.

Have I made it known widely, publicly, that I value this item on my twenty-loves list? Do my friends and associates know my preference here?

The point is that when we find something we "love to do" in our life but which we would *not* publicly affirm, our theory says it is not a value, but merely a value-*indicator*. This criterion causes a lot of difficulty for some people. But I always say to them, "We can remain silent about our value-indicators, but when something is a *value,* no one should doubt where we stand. They should be told, loudly and often.

Finally, if something is on our list of twenty things we love to do, it suggests we are, surely, already doing it, so it meets the seventh criterion. But if we haven't done it lately, then it does raise the question about whether or not it is a value or only a value-indicator. This criterion also argues eloquently for the notion that if something is a *value,* we can't merely mouth it, we have to *do* something about it.

Gestalt psychologists say that when someone claims he is "really going to do that some day," that person is actually saying, "I *won't* do that any day." If you are really going to do it, you would be doing it. Saying you are "really going to do it'" is equivalent to not doing it.

I would like to finish this with a strategy that you might do alone first, and then involve your family in when you're ready to include them. It's called Personal Coat of Arms.

Draw a shield about the size of this page. Divide it off into six more or less equal sections. What you are asked to do is to imagine this coat of arms on the wall right over the fireplace in your house, or emblazoned on the pocket of a blue blazer. It is your badge. It is your personal coat of arms.

For now, make a simple drawing in each section giving a symbolic representation for the required information. I ask for pictures because so many of us are facile with words.

1.   In section 1, list the thing that has been your greatest achievement up to this point in your life.

2. Draw a picture of the two things you think you are best at.
3. Draw a picture to show one thing about which you would never budge. This is one of the values you feel the strongest about.
4. Two more things you want out of life.
5. Draw a picture to show something you would do with your life if you could do anything you wanted to do and for which you would be guaranteed success.
6. Three words (and here is the only place on your coat of arms you use words) that you would like people to say about you after you are dead.

There is something very enlightening about looking at your coat of arms and thinking about what you stand for as a man or a woman. Each of us struggles to make something out of the fabric of our lives. We try to make meaning out of the sometimes overwhelming array of choices. An opportunity to reflect on what it all means is what the personal coat of arms supplies. One gratifying thing about it is that you can make a new coat of arms every few months. Our coat of arms changes as we change.

I said that it might be a good thing to get your family involved in the coat of arms with you. Work together to make a family coat of arms. Maybe that's the one that really should be above the fireplace. The questions are similar but are aimed at a family value-clarification experience. Here are some questions we've found useful for families:

1. What has been our family's greatest achievement?
2. What are two things we are good at as a family?
3. What would we like to stand for as a family, about which we would not budge?

4. What are two things we are struggling to become more of as a family?
5. What pain have we come through and overcome?
6. What are three words which we would like to be known for?

I hope this mini-course in values clarification has helped you. The search for all of us is long. To make sense out of this world of confusion and conflict is a full-time occupation. I take a great deal of comfort from the words of Dag Hammarskjöld: "Let me read with open eyes the book my days are writing—and learn."

Bibliography

While books and general articles dealing with many of the issues discussed in *Breaking Out* are available to even casual browsers, the papers listed below are not so well known and I list them for readers who wish to look further.

"Executive Counseling"
  Benjamin Balinsky, Bernard M. Baruch College, New York City.
"On the Death and Transfiguration of Leadership Training"
  Fred E. Fielder, Ph.D., University of Washington, Seattle, Washington.
"The Role of the Clinical Psychologist as Mediator Between the Organization and the Individual"
  Henry H. Morgan, PH.D., The Psychological Corporation, Princeton, New Jersey.
"Report of a Survey on Executive Tension in Business, 1971"
  Life Extension Institute, New York, N.Y.
"Selves and Selving: Development of a Sense of Self-Determination"
  Mary Ann Siderits, PH.D., Marquette University, Milwaukee, Wisconsin.
"The Humanistic Challenge to Society"
  John F. Glass, Ph.D., San Fernando State College, Northridge, California.

"The Ideal Self-Utilization Method"
   Herbert A. Otto, Ph.D., University of Utah, Salt Lake City,
   Utah
"Self-Determination and the Concept of Man"
   Louise Mead Riscalla, Ph.D., New Jersey State Diagnostic
   Center, Menlo Park, New Jersey.
"Prediction of Life Span"
   Erdman Palmore, Ph.D., Duke University, Durham, North
   Carolina
"Towards a Revolution in Industrial Psychology"
   Fred Massarick, Univ. of California at Los Angeles, Los
   Angeles, California.
"Is Life a Hereditary Disease?"
   Harold M. Vistosky, M.D., Northwestern University,
   Chicago, Illinois.
"Factors Related to How Superiors Establish Goals and Re-
view Performance For Their Subordinates"
   Stephen J. Carroll, Jr., and Dennis Cintron, University of
   Maryland, College Park, MD.,
   Henry Tossi, Michigan State University, East Lansing,
   Michigan.
"Organizational Change Through New Breeds of Employees:
The Potential of the Generation Gap"
   Douglas T. Hall, Ph.D., Yale University, New Haven, Con-
   necticut.
"The Future of Industrial Psychology: Oblivion or Millen-
nium?"
   Herbert H. Meyer, PH.D., General Electric, New York,
   N.Y.
"Organizational Climate: A View from the Change Agent"
   Michael Beer, Ph.D., Corning Glass Works, Corning, N.Y.
"Use Of Managers' Peer Ratings To Predict Executive Suc-
cess"
   Allen I. Kraut, Ph.D., IBM World Trade Corporation,
   New York, N.Y.

"Enchancing Attitude-Performance Relationships by Degree of Job Involvement"
    Donald A. Wood, Ph.D., Graduate School of Business, Indiana Univ., Bloomington, Indiana.
"Free Feels, Forced Fights and Phony Feelings"
    Bruce L. Maliver, Ph.D., Interaction Dynamics, Inc., New York, N.Y.
"Social Class Factors in Coping Style and Competence"
    Robert J. Havinghurst, Ph.D., University of Chicago, Chicago, Illinois.
"Effect of Site Plan and Social Status Variables on Distance to Friends' Homes"
    Gary A. Yoshioka and Robert B. Athanaslou, Johns Hopkins University, Baltimore, Maryland

9-28-73